SUBURBAN SURVIVAL

SUBURBAN SURVIVAL:

PREPARING FOR SOCIO-ECONOMIC COLLAPSE

REVISED AND UPDATED

JOE SNUFFY

WITH FORWARD BY

JAMES WESLEY, RAWLES

CreateSpace

CreateSpace.

Nonfiction / Reference / Publishing

Third Edition (March, 2017)

First Printing (September, 2012)

ISBN-13: 978-1490967059

ISBN-10: 1490967052

Printed in the United States by CreateSpace

Cover design and photos: Joe Snuffy

IMPORTANT NOTICE TO READERS:

As this book is instructional, some of the solutions to certain situations in this book are meant for a period in which a total degradation of society has occurred, such as the absence of all currently formal law enforcement, and the rule of law. Therefore, this book is written *for academic study only*.

This author will not have any liability or responsibility to any person or entity regarding any injury, loss or damage by the use of the contents of this book, by any person.

SUBURBAN SURVIVAL: PREPARING FOR SOCIO-ECONOMIC COLLAPSE

Table of Contents

Acknowledgments

I would like to acknowledge James Wesley, Rawles, at SurvivalBlog.com, the worlds' number one survivalism and preparedness website. Jim Rawles, himself a former US Army Intelligence Officer (We both went through the same schoolhouse, graduating with the same officer specialty exactly two decades apart. I got my commission late in my Army Reserve career), was the original inspiration for my dedication to preparedness, after Hurricane Katrina. I have always regretted having to kill my own website, and removing it from his blogroll (#2 from the top), but when it comes to OPSEC, I think Jim understands.

I would also like to mention other areas of inspiration. The late fictional writer and firearms expert Jerry Ahern comes to mind. One of his fictional series, *The Survivalist*, set off an entire sub-genre of post-apocalyptic fiction in the early 1980's, and helped to popularize the survivalism concept. I have fond memories of reading that series of novels while out in the field, serving as a young US Army Infantryman, in Alaska. In recent years, I have thought: "Why *couldn't* someone focus completely on being an ultra-survivalist, as in the form of the fictional John Thomas Rourke character?" James Rawles himself has already blazed that trail for us in the real world.

My thanks also go out to the Libyan people, who I got to meet while doing some freelance military journalism, and helping out in any small way that I could, during the Spring and Summer of 2011. The Libyan people have to be some of the most inviting, and thankful people on Earth. The Libyan Revolution of 2011 was a moment in history that I had to be a part of. Almost everyone I met, in every capacity, was helping the war effort, as if I had gone back in time to 1944 Europe, in the fight against the Nazis. This was not an "American Invasion," or "phony revolution," as some in the fringe media have called it. The Libyans were always concerned for my safety, from the time I arrived in Benghazi, to the incoming Grad missile and rifle fire I experienced on the front line, west of Misrata. What I saw there was a very self-reliant country, in terms of its relatively small population (only roughly six million), it's reserves of high-quality crude oil, agriculture, and other natural resources (even climate change seems to be working in the country's favor, as the Summer of 2011 there was actually the mildest in 30 years). My trip there helped to kick-start my professional writing career.

The late-2012 assassination of the US Ambassador in Benghazi was a tragic event, carried out by a radical fringe group, and was not representative of the Libyan people. It was a tragedy for them, in particular. Benghazi is the most pro-American city in North Africa, particularly while I had been there in 2011. While I was there, people were always asking me what us Americans thought of them, particularly since Gaddafi's shenanigans in the 1980's, which included invading neighbors, supporting virtually every terrorist group in Europe, killing American servicemen, etc (Sound familiar? The only difference is that in Gaddafi's case, it actually happened). I was constantly reassuring people there that Americans had no issues with the Libyan people, whatsoever.

I would like to thank my buddies Paul in Portland, Oregon, and D.C. in Grants Pass, Oregon, for their contributions to the individual tactical photo shoots.

Last, but by no means least, I'd like to thank my wife, the love of my life. She has always encouraged me as a writer (among other things, like getting more education, becoming a military officer, etc). Being a writer herself, her editing and PDF conversion work was instrumental in getting this book published.

Forward

by James Wesley, Rawles

Recent history has demonstrated that we live in an increasingly fragile society. As was evidenced by the earthquake, tsunami and subsequent Fukushima nuclear power plant disaster in Japan (in March of 2011), unexpected chains of events can have a profound effect on modern, technological societies, even to point of triggering a societal collapse.

We are now dependent upon power grids and telecommunication networks for nearly every aspect of our lives. Chains of supply for food and fuel span thousands of miles and we are dependent on computer-orchestrated "just in time" inventory control systems. The majority of our petrochemicals come from thousands of miles away--mostly from the war-torn Middle East. It doesn't take much to disrupt any of those, and once the disruption starts, things can come unraveled very rapidly. The aftermath of Hurricane Katrina in 2005 was clear evidence of that.

Hurricane Katrina was also evidence that governments are incapable of providing relief in disaster situations. In SurvivalBlog, this is what I call "YOYO" time—**you're on your own**!

I've just read the manuscript of *Suburban Survival: Preparing for Socio-Economic Collapse*. The book does an admirable job of teaching you how to prepare for and how to live through YOYO time, whether it is just 24 hours, or if it persists for many months. And it is notable that the sage teachings of this book are applicable to any nation that undergoes disruption

A variety of events can disrupt the fragile web that holds modern societies together. These events include: earthquakes, tsunamis, wildland fires, floods, tornadoes, hurricanes, naturally-occurring plagues, cyber attacks, terrorist nuclear, biological, or chemical attacks, economic spasms, and solar flares. These each have unique characteristics, but they all reveal the vulnerabilities of a society like our own.

Further exacerbating our predicament, modern societies have an increasingly stratified division of labor. In the early 20th Century, fully 20% of American families were employed at full-time farming, ranching, or fishing. But in the early 21st Century, just 2% of the population feeds the other 98%. Think about the implications of that. If we were to experience a repeat of The Great Depression in today's world, how long would it be before we reached the point of societal collapse?

Prepared individuals size up the potential threats and take active measures to insure the health and safety of themselves and their family members. Steps as simple as buying a compact water filter and laying in a several month supply of food can make a tremendous difference between being a survivor, and being a statistic. This book is chock full of practical steps that will keep you and your loved ones from assuming room temperature.

Like me, "Joe Snuffy" had training as a military intelligence officer, and similarly had the opportunity to work in a variety of intelligence-related environments. This experience left an indelible mark on him, and helped to shape his worldview. Among other things, working those real world intel missions gave him a profound appreciation of the fragility of modern societies.

Mr. Snuffy has the rare gift of being able to study complex situations, analyze risks and variables, and then formulate truly practical courses of action. He has the mind of both a tactician and a strategist. Few men can embody both, at least at his advanced level. His knowledge is not just theoretical. Mr. Snuffy succeeds at bridging the gaps between theory and practice, between intellectual discourse, and pulling the trigger, to dispense hot lead.

He can, and *has*, done it all.

Snuffy has led a life that has been both physically and mentally vigorous. In his many "past lives", he has been an active duty military intelligence officer, professional writer, freelance military journalist, electronics technician, and a preparedness consultant. He has served various tours in his former US Army Reserve status. Most recently, he traveled to Libya, at the height of the civil war, shortly after the No-Fly Zone was declared, in order to offer his assistance, and to document his experiences, as he went from living with the Libyan Rebel Army in Benghazi, to being under fire west of Misrata, after the siege of that city.

I'd like to be able to tell you more about Mr. Snuffy's varied background, but that would create the risk of revealing his identity. I suppose that those details must remain *sub rosa* until Mr. Snuffy reaches a ripe old age and can tell it all. What a tale that will be!

In the chapters ahead, you will learn about Peak Oil and the many other risks that could plunge First World countries into the depths of societal collapse. Then, going beyond mere "what if" conjecture, the book provides truly *practical and tactical* solutions to keeping yourself alive in the most traumatic times imaginable. This book covers the gamut of topics from personal finances to food storage, martial arts, home security, firearms, camouflage, barter, bug out bags, and survival strategies.

We live in an uncertain world that now teeters on the brink of economic collapse. In his writings, Mr. Snuffy authoritatively removes some of those uncertainties. For that, we are in his debt.

James Wesley, Rawles

The Rawles Ranch

July, 2012

Author's Preface

This is the third edition of *Suburban Survival: Preparing for Socio-Economic Collapse*. As I explained in the conclusion of the first edition of this book, I was required to do a rush job on the first edition. The release of this book in time for fall, 2012 was imperative, due to several different unique events that were converging during that time. There are now a new set of events:

- The latest 2016 presidential election. Trump himself is a threat to the "Deep State," within the U.S. Government. This in itself could end in an outright coup, or assassination. Objectively speaking as a collapse theorist, I believe (at the time of this update) that what President Trump represents is somewhat of a planned simplification of things in this country, through deregulation. As Ancient Rome had been undergoing centuries of decline (much of which had been due to over-complexity. The U.S. after 9/11 is a perfect example), there were one, maybe two emperors who had managed to reform things, to even include their perpetually inflating currency![1] Unplanned simplification is the definition of collapse (Tainter). Distant historians (if there are any) may likely see Trump's presidency as a period of reform, that kept the American Empire running a little longer, before its ultimate collapse.

- Mass migrations, due to resource depletion and climate change. At the time of this writing (FEB 2017), California has been experiencing flooding not seen in decades. Prior to this, it was in the grip of an epic drought. Europe has

---

[1]   Something the U.S. has yet to do, particularly since removing itself from The Gold Standard. One unnerving difference between us and Rome.

been inundated with refugees from the Middle East. The Summer temperatures in that part of the world in 2016 were the highest on record. Also, declining oil production in Syria[2], along with its worst drought in history were the original issues that led to that country's civil war.

I had originally been approached for this book by a certain magazine (using their branding for the book) and the conventional publisher that they were working with. I was extremely flattered to be approached with this idea by this particular magazine. It was like a teenage dream come true! However, delays would have kept my original book from being published until February, 2013. As many are now aware within our society, there was no guarantee that we would even get to February, 2013. After this, and other conflicts (such as being misinformed regarding what illustrations I could not use from the public domain, the titling of the book, etc.), I sent their advance payment back, and terminated my contract with said publisher.

One thing that the reader of this book can feel good about is that this book was printed in the good old U.S. of A. The recent trend in self-publishing has created a new industry, forcing books to be printed *within* the US. The original publisher who I wrote this manuscript for regularly has their books printed in China, .

I was very happy with my original cover image. I had a strong image of what I wanted the cover photo to look like, so I thought I would keep it for the second edition. I wanted the cover to grab people's attention, as well as helping the reader to visualize the

---

2   Syria's oil production had peaked in 1996.

tactical aspects of immediate post-collapse living, as Jim Rawles himself had described in his groundbreaking manual dressed-as-fiction *Patriots: A Novel of Survival in the Coming Collapse*. I also like the image from Rawles' recent book *Founders*, of a certain pair of characters in full ruck, with weapons and ammunition. This image should help serve as a wake-up call for all of the armchair survivalists out there...

The initial reviews on Amazon of my previous edition were somewhat negative, to say the least. Looking at the review history at Amazon of the individuals who made these reviews, it is apparent that I offended the people who resembled my remarks: The mall ninjas, zombie apocalypse types, chubby wannabes', etc. I clearly stated that my book, despite its forward by Jim Rawles, was not intended to be the end-all and know-all of preparedness and survivalism. It was intended for the general public, as a handy, physical form of reference. They may have also been offended by various aspects of my book, as it forces people who may feel that they are well-prepped, to take a step back, and think about certain reality issues, such as physical fitness, debt reduction, etc. If some people were looking for newly invented wiz-bang aspects of survivalism and self-reliance, they were out of luck. After several millennia of collapsed civilizations, we humans already have this knowledge. I'm just simply re-presenting this information in a more compact physical form, by focusing on its core aspects.

Based on my experience with people at various public events such as flea markets, preparedness expos', etc., I wanted to target the general public, on-up. The timing here is perfect: A growing majority of the general public now acknowledges the possibility of societal collapse. At these public events, my first edition was very well received, with many people leaving positive comments.

Yes, granted, most of the information in this book can be accessed from the web, from websites like SurvivalBlog.com, or from YouTube. What my book does is package the information in a handy, small, non-volatile form of memory called "a book." Writers from each end of the societal doomer spectrum, from the climate change and peak oil neo-hippies (who know a lot about the theoretical science of civilizational collapse, but do not know much about actual preparedness) to the bible-thumping, mass-quantities-of-firepower survivalists (who know *a lot* about preparedness, but do not necessarily believe in climate change or peak oil), have strongly recommended putting all of your reference material into hard copies. When the bad times come and you're hunkered down and locked and loaded, a good way to spend time (if you have any) is to read from hard print (or your computer, if you have the information stored, with your own power generation), and review your preps, procedures, etc.

I hope you enjoy this third edition of *Suburban Survival: Preparing for Socio-Economic Collapse*!

Joe Snuffy

March, 2017

I.   Introduction: Why This Book?

At this point in time, there is no need to wake people up, or remind them that we are now in a period of socio-economic decline. Everyone now knows, or at least senses it, from the average uneducated layman, to the intellectuals who have studied peak oil, climate change, fiat based currency, etc. (as well as their combined effects). These crises are in addition to a slew of global sub-crises, such as exponential human population growth, the loss of topsoil, beehive colony collapse disorder, etc.

There are two distinct forms of societal collapse, known as the slow crash, and the fast crash.

The slow crash represents what we've been in since the early 1970's, when we started hitting road bumps, such as the peaking of US oil production in December of 1970 at roughly 9.5 mbl/d (million barrels per day). In 1971, President Nixon removed the last vestiges of the gold standard from the US Dollar ("we won't just print more money, trust us") as a result of US foreign debt, brought on by The Vietnam War and the US Space Program. The 1973 Arab Oil Embargo woke up the US, making it realize then that we imported roughly a third of our oil from foreign sources, at that time (we now import roughly half). Average wages, wealth disparity, and quality of life indicators have been on the decline since.

Granted, there have been periods of recovery and economic growth, such as oil production coming on-line in the early-1980's from non-OPEC sources, such as The North Sea, Alaska, and Mexico's supergiant Cantarell oil field, effectively taking pricing power away from the Arabs, and OPEC (it was NOT due to the so-called Reagan-Thatcherite Era). The end of the Cold War, the manipulation of interest rates in the mid-to-late 1990's, along

1

with the dot.com bubble and the IT industry's preparations for Y2K created prosperity at that time.

However, there are no giant oil fields left to discover in the Western Hemisphere, as discoveries measured in billions of barrels peaked in the mid-1960's, according to both the International Energy Agency (IEA), and the US Energy Information Agency (US EIA, the information arm of the US Dept. of Energy). Central banks around the world have dropped their interest rates to zero, or near zero (The US Federal Reserve's rate now sits at one quarter of one percent). Central banks and governments are now running out of options, with which to continue running the global debt-based financial system, other than to create more debt through "quantitative easing," robbing individual savings accounts in certain countries (as with Cyprus, in 2013), etc. There is a direct relationship between cheap, accessible energy (the 2006 peak/plateau in world oil production), and continuing global economic growth.

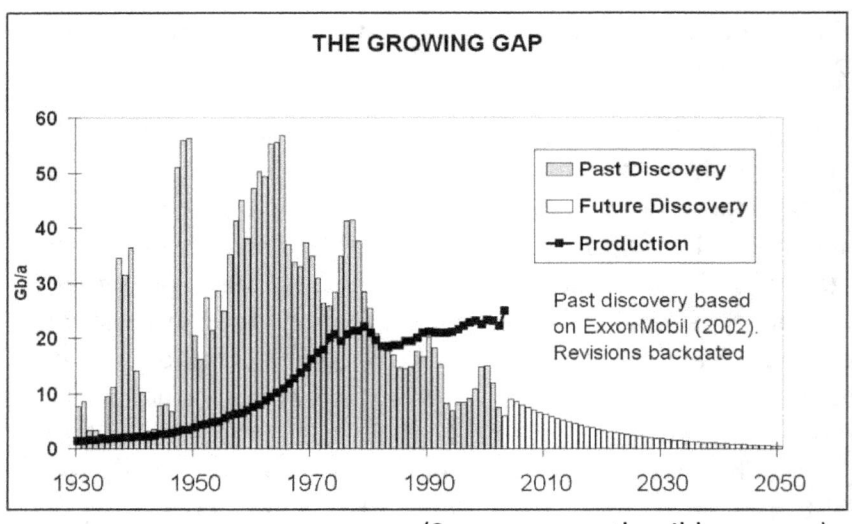

THE GROWING GAP

(Source: www.theoildrum.com)

This chart from 2002 shows the amount of crude oil discovered in billions of barrels per year. Discoveries clearly peaked back in the mid-1960's, due to discoveries in The North Sea and Alaska, in particular.

The fast crash represents something a little more exciting, such as something you would see from a movie. The fast crash would be in the form of a sudden emergency, such as the sudden collapse of the dollar, or of the entire global financial system (we were reportedly just hours away from a collapse of the entire global banking system, during the Fall of 2008). A fast crash would also happen on the regional level, from a natural or man-made disaster (Hurricane's Katrina and Sandy, the tsunami and nuclear disaster at Fukushima). However, most regional disasters can be recovered from, *to some extent*. As of this writing, there has been no complete recovery from any of the recent major US hurricanes, or the ongoing disaster at Fukushima.

Other examples of a fast crash would include a nuclear war, a massive asteroid collision, an electrical magnetic pulse (EMP) event that affects an entire hemisphere (if not the entire planet), etc.

Kathy McMahon, of PeakOilblues.com describes what we are in, in the United States, as the "sucky collapse," where instead of dramatic calamities, we experience job layoffs, lower-paying jobs, and declining standards of living. This, most realistically, is the type of collapse that I am trying to help people prepare for, with this book.

After all, this is the year 2013. Weren't we already supposed to have flying cars, vacations in space, and a *real* space station, like the permanent one in the movie *2001: A Space Odyssey* (or the sequel *2010: The Year We Make Contact*, which came out in the 1980's)? It seems that the Soviet Union were the only ones who could put a semi-permanent space station (Mir) in orbit, while all the US could do during the 1980's was to put out propaganda, by ending each news story done on Mir with the phrase "...the troubled space station."

And the hits just keep on coming. Due to the crises of the US federal debt and budget deficit, there is no more manned US Space Program for the foreseeable future. At the time of this writing, American astronauts are hitching rides with the Russians, in order to exchange crews at the International Space Station, which is scheduled to be de-funded (if not de-orbited) by 2020. The Apollo Moon landings were truly "the pyramids" of our current, globalized civilization.

Or, even better, weren't we supposed to cure all diseases by now, including cancer? Currently being suppressed by the medical industry is the fact that there are nutritional treatments for cancer, with a high rate of success, which have been suppressed for decades, such as the work conducted by the Gerson Institute.

Charles Eisenstein, in his brilliant work *The Ascent of*

Humanity (subtitled *The Age of Separation, the Age of Reunion, and the Convergence of Crises that is birthing the transition*) is one of very few writers who have made readers aware of this realization. From Chapter One of his book:

> The 1960's were in many ways the summit of our civilization. We had beaten polio, smallpox and plague. Surely cancer and the rest would succumb in due course. We had beaten the Nazis. Surely the Commies were next to go. Social problems like poverty, racism, illiteracy, racism, crime and mental illness would be engineered out of existence. Everything pointed to unlimited growth and continued triumph: atomic power, robots, space, artificial intelligence, maybe even immortality. But in the words of Patrick Farley, the future has been running a little behind schedule.

In other words, the idea that "humans are evolving," as Gene Roddenberry liked to say at various *Star Trek* conventions does not appear to be happening (or at least not fast enough). While it may be happening on a small scale (such as the Occupy Movement, the current "back to the land" and other progressive movements), we still seem to be suffering from greed, war, imperialism, etc.

Due to the rate at which events are now taking place, I have concluded that the priority of situations that we currently have to deal with consist of the following:

- The continuing global debt crisis, which started with the US financial collapse of 2008. This ongoing crisis could result in the end of global economic growth in-itself, sooner than the 2030 figure given by the 1972 MIT / Club of Rome's *Limits to Growth* study. As I describe in this chapter, the original 1972 study's data has recently been revisited, and is still tracking on-schedule. The premise of perpetual economic growth is flawed anyway, since there is nothing wrong with a steady-state economy, as it has existed for much of the history of human civilization.

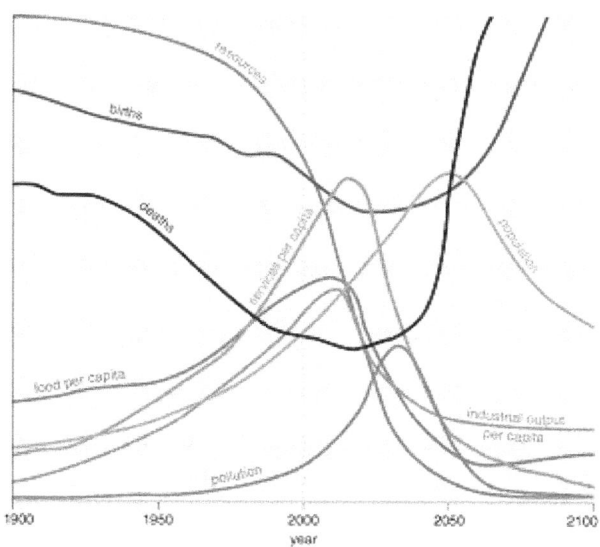

Trend chart from the 1972 MIT computer-modeled study _Limits to Growth_, commissioned by _The Club of Rome_. This published study has been revisited by scientists in its 40th Anniversary. The data is shockingly accurate and is still tracking on-schedule, indicating the complete end of world economic growth by the year 2030 (From _Revisiting the Limits to Growth After Peak Oil_, American Scientist Online).

- Climate change. October 2012's Hurricane Sandy devastated New York and New Jersey, turning more of the US population into true believers, regarding climate change. Due to the ongoing US government budget crisis, it took over two months for the US Congress to authorize funds for the recovery from this storm (it only took *five* days, after Hurricane Katrina), and did not include any funding for building seawalls, future flood protection, etc. In addition, an even deadlier storm, Typhoon Bopha occurred in the southern Philippines, roughly one month later. Although storms regularly reach this area, Typhoon Bopha was the most southerly typhoon ever recorded in the western Pacific.

While some of the more hardcore, religion-based survivalists out there may not believe in this concept, there are some non-debatable facts regarding the history of declines in the rate of oil production.

Domestic US oil production peaked at roughly 9.5 mbl/d (million barrels per day) in December, 1970, and despite some temporary increase in production in the 1980's from Alaskan oil production, has gone into long-term decline (without going into detail, at roughly 7 mbl/day, we now produce what we once did during WWII. In other words, at roughly 18 mbl/d consumption, US energy independence is a *fantasy*). This includes the North Slope of Alaska, which previously peaked in the late 1980s at roughly two mbl/d, and now produces a little over 600,000 bl/d.

As for unconventional oil, the shale plays in the U.S. are literally a mirage. Yes, they are currently (as of 2012) producing roughly 600,000 bl/d, and could possibly ramp-up, to a peak of three million bl/d. However, this is all based on the latest "fraking" technology (and is expensive), which means that the other side of the production profile chart for this oil play could drop like a rock (which is predicted by many Peak Oil theorists).

However, I would be the first to admit that the slowdown in the global economy has slowed-down the rate of oil consumption, primarily within the US. This is known in Peak Oil circles as *demand destruction*. Therein lies the rub: As we sit on this "bumpy plateau," even if a given recession does bottom-out, then begin to recover, high oil prices will kill any subsequent economic growth.

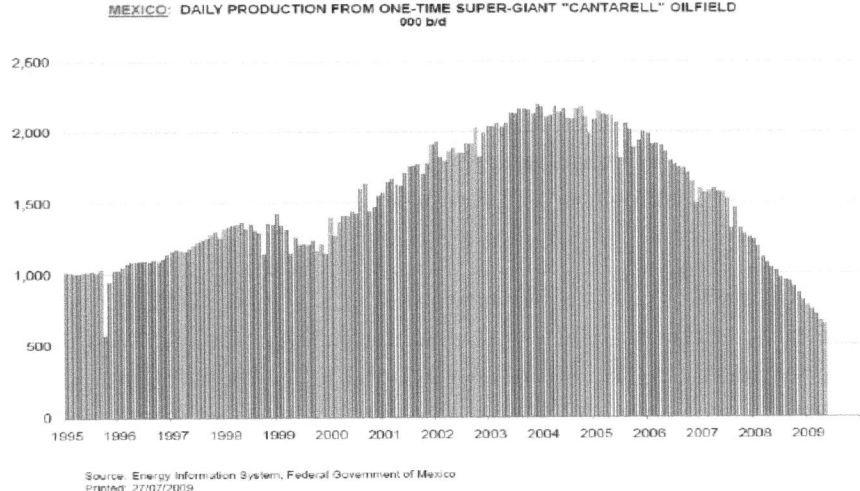

MEXICO: DAILY PRODUCTION FROM ONE-TIME SUPER-GIANT "CANTARELL" OILFIELD
000 b/d

Source: Energy Information System, Federal Government of Mexico
Printed: 27/07/2009

(Source: www.theoildrum.com)

This production profile chart of Mexico's giant Cantarell oil field (the largest in the Western Hemisphere) shows a dramatic decline in daily oil production, from a peak of roughly 2.2 mbl/day in 2004, to roughly 700,000 bl/day, by 2009. These year-over-year declines are occurring in oilfields around the world, particularly the fields that have been on-line for decades, such as The North Sea, Prudhoe Bay (Alaska), and various fields throughout The Middle East. In terms of energy density, there are currently no combinations of alternative energies that can run our current industrialized civilization.

Indeed, my primary reasons for becoming a full-blown survivalist in recent years are not just based on my research into our current debt-based economic system, climate change and resource depletion, but from my recollections from being in California's foster care system. This society's reactions to these issues are the part that concerns me. During the hard economic times of the 1970's, to make a long story short, I ended-up without parents, relatives, etc. as of age 11. I ended-up in a foster home that was run by an outright predator, sadist, and drug addict. These are the types of people who will come out of the woodwork as socio-economic decline continues (not to mention a "fast crash" scenario). Imagine what happens when these people go without a few meals, and are not held in-check by people who represent force, or the threat of force, which ultimately is the only thing that human beings in our society seem to understand.

Unlike the survival TV shows that you see on The Discovery Channel, I do not expect all the readers of this book to live in, or near wilderness. The intent of this book is to teach real-world practical skills for surviving socio-economic decline, if not outright upheaval, regardless of where you live, since most of us live in an urban, or suburban setting.

Dmitry Orlov's Five Stages of Collapse

Dmitry Orlov (www.cluborlov.com) has done brilliant work in his comparative analysis of the collapse of the Soviet Union, and American prospects. Born in Leningrad (now Saint Petersburg), Orlov originally came to the US at the age of 12, and traveled back-and-forth between the US and Russia before, during, and after the fall of the Soviet Union. However, as Orlov is a member of the fringe collection of doomer intellectuals, I do not agree with some of his other bastardized theories about US Foreign Policy. For instance, having been in Libya during its 2011 Revolution, I can vouch for the fact that *it was not* a "phony revolution," engineered by the United States.

In his somewhat small, yet brilliant book *Reinventing Collapse: The Soviet Union and American Prospects,* Orlov describes the advantages that the Soviet Union had, such as public transportation and public property, as compared to the US, where everything is based on the car, and private property. As he also describes the effects of Peak Oil in the book, he also states his theory of the five stages of societal collapse:

> Stage One: Financial collapse. Faith in "business as usual" is lost. The future is no longer assumed to resemble the past in any way that allows risk to be assessed and financial assets to be guaranteed. Financial institutions become insolvent; savings are wiped out, and access to capital is lost.
>
> Stage Two: Commercial collapse. Faith that "the market shall provide" is lost. Money is devalued and/or becomes scarce, commodities are hoarded, import and retail chains break down, and widespread shortages of survival necessities become the norm.
>
> Stage Three: Political collapse. Faith that "the government will take care of you" is lost. As official attempts to mitigate widespread loss of access to commercial sources of survival necessities fail to make a difference, the political establishment loses legitimacy and relevance.
>
> Stage Four: Social collapse. Faith that "your people will take care of you" is lost, as local social

institutions, be they charities or other groups that rush in to fill the power vacuum run out of resources or fail through internal conflict.

Stage Five: Cultural collapse. Faith in the goodness of humanity is lost. People lose their capacity for "kindness, generosity, consideration, affection, honesty, hospitality, compassion, charity" (Turnbull, *The Mountain People*). Families disband and compete as individuals for scarce resources. The new motto becomes "May you die today so that I die tomorrow" (Solzhenitsyn, *The Gulag Archipelago*). There may even be some cannibalism.

In a February 2012 interview with Max Keiser, Dmitry Orlov stated he believes that Stages One through Three are now happening simultaneously, within the US.

Looking back on it, I could even say that Stage Five occurred for me, at the personal level, back in the 1970's. After I was removed from my abusive father, then relinquished from him in 1976 at the age of 11, no relatives from either side of my family chose to show any concern, at all. Back then (like now), the scarce resources were jobs, money, etc. Therefore, the rest of my childhood was spent in California's foster care system.

In all, this book will place emphasis on the most basic fundamental components of preparedness and survivalism, as this book is not only intended as reflection for the experienced survivalist, but for the entire spectrum of the current preparedness movement: Everyone from the more intellectual "granola eating" eco-happy types (i.e., the ones who are fans of websites like *The Automatic Earth*, *Resilience.org*, etc.,) to experienced, and seasoned survivalists (the ones who have

SurvivalBlog.com as their home page, for example).

Those fundamental components are as follows (in order of importance):

- Debt elimination and economic survival
- Physical fitness
- Nutrition
- Elimination of clutter (an epidemic within the American lifestyle). This affects the ability to store needed goods within your home (to include people if / when you "double-up"). It also affects your ability to move around quickly within and around your home
- Overall self-reliance (or distancing yourself from "the grid" and the monetized economy, as much as possible)

No book can prepare everyone for every given scenario, or situation. This is why this book focuses on the core components of preparedness, and survivalism. In any given emergency or crisis, people will have to think on their feet, as they make decisions, and prioritize, based on their own situations. One thing that I learned from the military is that a 75%-correct decision made quickly, is better than a 100%-correct decision made too late.

We need to understand that there are two basic forms of collapse: Societal, and personal. The one term that defines societal collapse is an unplanned *simplification*. This is what occurred, after all, when the Roman Empire collapsed, or the Mayan civilization for that matter, when everyone basically just headed back into the rain forest.

As for myself, I try to live a continually improving life, full of social capital (family and friends), physical capital (being healthy, and staying at a certain level of physical fitness), and fiscal capital (financial resources, assets, savings, avoidance of all debt, bills, etc.). Indeed, I personally view the modern survivalism / preparedness movement primarily *as a vehicle for one's own continual self-improvement.*

II   Economic Preparedness

"Study your math, kids. It's the key to the universe."

- Christopher Walken as the archangel Gabriel from the movie
The Prophecy (1995)

a. Creating an Economic Bunker

This is actually the most important aspect of this book. Many preppers who have jumped on the preparedness bandwagon in recent years have been clueless in my opinion, due to the fact that they acknowledge having bought beans, bullets and band-aids, yet lost their house and vehicles, due to job losses from the current economic decline.

What in God's name did these people actually think that they were prepping *for*? Folks, *right now*: If you owe money on credit cards, vehicles, your house, etc, then you're not prepped.

Before you start getting images of emulating Charlton Heston from *The Omega Man*, you need to understand that we still live in this little thing called *the real world*, and in this world is this thing called *the Dollar*, which is currently still worth something. Hopefully, you are not being too influenced by all the fringe doomers out there on the internet, who keep reminding everyone that the Dollar is about to collapse, either next week, next month, or this year.

This message goes out to all the people who are fortunate enough to still have jobs, along with their Brady Bunch McHouses / McMansions, living the soccer mom lifestyle. If you are one job loss away from losing all this, then you need to (as of yesterday) stop spending money on everything as it relates to prepping: No more beans, bullets, or band-aids, or that piston-operated AR-15 rifle, that you've been drooling over at each gun show you attend (and without experience or training with military-style weapons, it's not going to do you any good, anyway). In addition, many of the skills and techniques in this book do not require any money being spent.

If you're divorced, widowed, been swindled out of your life savings, etc, these are forms of personal collapse. However, like many localized natural or man-made disasters, these can be recovered from.

And speaking of personal collapse, I would like to address something that sounds sexist, but this an important issue, if you want to avoid personal collapse in your own lives. I have seen this repeated in other family's lives, as well as having had this occur in my own, at a young age:

To all of the families still living in NFL/NASCAR/Disneyland world, this message goes out to all the wives (and OK, maybe *some* husbands) out there: Quit bugging your spouse about moving-up to a bigger/nicer house! I think we've all seen the manipulative TV commercial that ran during the sub-prime housing boom of the 2000's, where this pushy little mutt of a wife gets in her husband's face and tells him, "I want that house!"

This ruins families! In my own experience, in 1971, when I was six years old, because of my mom's insistence, we moved to a brand new house, with central air conditioning, and even a powerful central vacuum system, where you simply plug the vacuum hose into a receptacle in each room. State-of-the-art, even by modern standards!

When my family made this move, we ended-up leaving a neighborhood where we had a real community: We baby-sat each other's kids, helped each other work on their cars, etc: All of the services that our society now monetizes. Not only that, but we lived close enough to the oil refinery where my father worked, to where he could get there by bicycle. Our newer house was at least

15 miles away, accessible only by a freeway that was known for its accidents, at that time.

Needless to say, our new neighborhood had no community, whatsoever. Not only that, but for some reason, my father had difficulty affording this newer house, and three years later, we sold the house, and rented after that. It was during this time, in 1975, that my mother basically drank herself to death, which ultimately led to me entering California's foster care system.

Years ago, even my own lovely wife was talking about us moving-up to a larger, newer house, in the mid 2000's (telling me that her family would even expect that of her!). At that time I explained to her that we were in the midst of a housing and debt bubble that was set to implode, and that we would end-up being underwater with the newer mortgage, when housing values began dropping.

Fast-forward to just a few years later, and my wife agreed with me that I was right.

Damn, I just hate being right all the time!

As someone who has been actively prepping since about Hurricane Katrina, societal collapse does not bother me that much, in itself. I know it is coming, and that it is a natural part of the human experience, for the last roughly 10,000 years of human civilization. We are simply too young a species, and have not evolved enough within this time period to make any given civilization work. In case you haven't noticed, and as I have already alluded to, we're currently repeating all of the mistakes of previous civilizations: Centralization of power in the hands of individuals with short-term interests, imperialism, greed, warfare, the mismanagement of declining resources, etc.

I'm actually looking forward to it. It is basically a transition, in which I plan to thrive, on the other side. Some people might be jealous, however, which is why I try to maintain a low profile, and have weapons.

My advice for those who consider themselves preppers (and are aware that they are living in a constructed dream world: The "American lifestyle") consists of the following:

Get out of all debt, starting with credit cards, then vehicles, then your house, depending on where you're at in the mortgage. As economic decline (i.e., deflation) gets worse, debt elimination is imperative. To achieve this, I recommend pulling all money out of your investments, including employer-provided retirement plans, such as IRA's, 401K's and state employment "457" funds, if possible. If recently laid-off, this should be no problem. Just take the tax hit, and get out. By paying off debt, you will actually save (more like make) yourself tens of thousands of dollars (By the way, have you ever actually looked at an amortization schedule, and seen how much money lenders actually make off of you?). As of now, you and your children should plan on lives without credit. Certain religious orders, such as the Amish, Mennonites, New Brethren Order, etc, do not even allow the use of debt, and are pretty well-off, as a result. You will not find any lending institutions in those areas, because there is simply no way for them to make any money.

The only time where debt has been a virtue was during times of hyperinflation, as had occurred in Weimar Germany, where people paid off business and home loans, with just a postage stamp. We are not there yet. However, as the US Federal Reserve continues to prop-up the economy artificially with money printing ("Quantitative Easing," or the non-stop monetizing of debt, as of this writing), we could see some form of mass-inflation, in the not-to-distant future.

Greece is a perfect example of socio-economic collapse. Every single public and private institution is in debt: The socialized medical system is in debt, therefore people are not getting necessary prescription drugs, to include even aspirin! The electrical utility there has even stated that there may be indefinite power outages, because they are in debt, and cannot make regular payments to Greece's natural gas company (who themselves are in debt, and where do they ultimately get *their* natural gas? Russia's Gazprom! And as history has taught us, when the Russians have the advantage, they do not negotiate), from which their electrical power is generated. Just about every private company in Greece is in debt, and begging their business-to-business ("B to B") customers to make payments, but they can't because they're in debt, too! More recently, there is even news of potential food shortages (Yes, without "letters of credit," even here in the US, the trucks could cease backing up to the loading docks at your local Wal-Mart).There is just no liquidity in Greece, and analyst / activists like Nicole Foss (aka, "Stoneleigh," along with her writing partner "Ilargi"), who has been preaching a coming global liquidity crisis and resulting deflation (i.e., deflation, as in the 1930's Great Depression, except this time much worse) at her website *The Automatic Earth*, is having the mother of all "I told you so's" (They also predicted the equities and commodities crash that occurred in July, 2008).

Nowadays, you don't have to go to the fringe internet community for "doomer porn." Just go to CSPAN, where our federal government now openly discusses fiscal collapse (which technically has never happened before in our nation's history), along with references to cutting long established social services (Medicare, social security, etc), and imposing austerity. I was getting this predictive intel at least five years ago, so I am not shocked by these discussions.

While paying off all debt, you can then focus on the other things that do not require (much) money. Things like organic gardening (and building topsoil!), food preservation, improving the physical security around your house, free skills training provided by various organizations, the removal of clutter from inside / outside your home, and garage (it's difficult to move fast during an emergency, in a cluttered-up house. Also, you may need the extra space to store supplies, as well as additional people.

Think minimalist-style, Fung Shuay, etc). These things will all be covered in subsequent chapters.

Once you are out of debt: Tangibles, tangibles, tangibles, as Jim Rawles at SurvivalBlog.com has put to the forefront of everyone's attention. Jim Rawles' advice over the years has actually been the best investment advice I've ever received. This would be the time to stock up on your beans, bullets and band-aids. In fact, at the time of this writing, the price of 9mm pistol ammunition has dropped back down to as low as $9.00 / 50 round box (equivalent). At the height of the Obama election / gun rights scare in the fall of 2008, the same box of 9mm ammo was selling for as much as $16.00.

Even if societal collapse does not come, price inflation always will. There was an excellent book written in 1980 called *The Alpha Strategy: The Ultimate Plan of Financial Self-Defense*, by John A. Pugsley. This book is also available as a free PDF download. This book could have been written last year, as Pugsley spends most of the time describing the world financial situation since 1971, when President Nixon took the US Dollar off of the last vestiges of the gold standard. Pugsley illustrated the increasing rate (at that time, not to mention at present) of US Government national debt, and its implications. Towards the end of his book, Pugsley finally goes into his strategy, of buying everyday items, paper products, automotive products, etc. in bulk, and stockpiling them, if you have the space. He also presents data on the value per cubic foot, of various items.

Table 2

Item	Value per Cubic Foot
Viva paper towels	4.10
Purina dog chow	6.10
Northern toilet tissue	6.20
Kleenex	10.50
Comet cleanser	12.20
Joy dishwashing liquid	15.30
Wheat	17.20
Cascade dishwasher detergent	27.60
Tires (HR-70/15 steel radial)	28.10
G.E. lightbulbs	30.50
Camay bath soap	61.00
Smirnoff vodka	112.70
Aluminum foil (12" x 1,000')	123.00
Gillette Trac II razor blades	845.00

Value per cubic foot of storage (in 1980 USD) from *The Alpha Strategy* (1980)

Although the book itself is a little dated, to say the least (nobody I know has used Gillette Trac II blades in at least 20 years), the information is literally timeless, as you can see the authors logic. This type of information is critical, not only for organizing our own storage space, but for storing barterables. Who wouldn't want things like vodka, bourbon, and tequila, in well-known and high-end brands, after a societal collapse? Although this book was written during the first round of popularity into the modern survivalist movement, Pugsley was not a survivalist, *per se*. He was definitely thinking economic preparedness, however.

The previous table is just a simple guide. At present, and in terms of the value per cubic foot, I believe that the three best things to stockpile for purely financial purposes at the moment, in order of importance are: Common caliber firearm ammunition, physical cash, and physical silver.

Ammunition is ideal; regardless of whether-or-not you have the firearms for these calibers. Store common calibers such as .45 ACP, 9mm, 5.56mm (.223), 7.62 NATO (.308), 7.62x39mm (Russian AK ammunition), and 7.62x54r (Mosin-Nagant rifle).

And yes, .40 cal. S&W (Smith & Wesson) pistol ammunition. I fail to understand this pistol cartridge's huge popularity. I hate that caliber, and fail to understand why there has to be a bastardized "in-between" caliber between European 9mm and good old, uniquely American .45 ACP (the domestic US handgun industry has been working on an "in-between" cartridge since the 1980's, to the point where 10mm pistol ammunition turned into a fad that came, and went). This round is no more effective in killing and maiming people than any other large-caliber automatic pistol cartridge (research conducted decades ago by the US Army concluded that *shot placement* is more important than caliber).

In Bosnia in the 1990's for instance, ammunition *was* the currency (especially inside the besieged city of Sarajevo), and was actually in short supply, compared to the number of actual weapons that were floating around before, and during the conflict (the area of Serbo-Croatia has always had a very strong gun culture). Ammunition is already commonly used in the US as a form of currency, as people trade it for weapons, gunsmithing services, and even non-firearms related barter (using the current US dollar value as a relative guide, of course). Needless to say, ammunition *will* be the currency, if we have a complete, grid-down societal collapse. At present, I do not see the price of ammunition going any lower, so stock-up now!

Having physical cash on hand is smart, in the event that a severe liquidity crisis happens here (more like *when* it happens to the US), to the point where ATM's no longer dispense cash, or in very small amounts per account holder. It's also great to have on hand for any local regional disasters, such as earthquakes, tornadoes, etc. In addition, as socio-economic conditions worsen in the US and we become more-and-more of a police state (until governments finally go bankrupt; anyway), physical cash is the best way to keep Big Brother guessing about your financial activities.

Precious metals have always been used as a hedge against inflation. If the US Dollar does lose value, as many predict (but not anytime soon, based on our more obvious trending towards deflation), then physical silver will be sought-after. Gold, at present prices of over $1500/oz. is too compact for normal barter, unless you buy it in one-tenth of an ounce coins. Only invest in them while the US Dollar is still worth *something*. Try to buy them during periods of correction, or "on the dips." For those who like to trade, short-term money can also be made currently on silver, by tracking its price, just as with any stock.

However, do not put all of your hopes in precious metals. As I mention in other parts of this book, if you can't eat it, wear it, or shoot it, you should not place that much emphasis on it. Also, do your research, in learning how to conceal, or secretly cache valuables in, and around your house. There is a plethora of information and products available on the internet that allow for very creative solutions for hiding cash, precious metals, etc., in-and-around your house. In other words, *be your own bank*.

At this point, another good step would be to invest in some land, for "recreational purposes." If you can buy a rural house away from it all as Rawles suggests, as your rural retreat, then you need to make sure that someone is watching, or living at the property 24/7, otherwise it is a given that it will be vandalized and ransacked. My ultimate idea here would be to buy a piece of property, dig a giant trench, and drop either a pre-fabbed concrete root cellar, or the pre-fabbed tubular survival shelters, now being offered from several different companies. While there is no guarantee of complete OPSEC here, something like this would be easy to physically conceal, in order to have pre-positioned supplies at your retreat property. Then later, if you have already bugged out, and are living at your new doomstead, you could then build additionally on top of that. I do not believe we are nearing a point where an underground bunker would be needed (or useful for that matter) in-itself, but as a way to conceal a structure on remote property, it works.

Another main use for this land would be to practice your weapons and tactical skills: Marksmanship, using cover and concealment, moving with a rifle, buddy team and fire team drills. Remember, as survivalists, we should not see assault rifles as cool-looking toys. Just as professional Army and Marine infantrymen, we should see them as workout tools.

When picking land for this purpose, these four factors should be considered:

- Access to water: A nearby river, an existing well, or at least the prioritized plan of sinking a well. Or, depending on your region, a pond, or rainwater cistern.
- Defendability: No more than one way in, or out by road (virtually everyone, including our own military, are incredibly road-bound), with the back of a property against a river, or some other type of restrictive land formation.
- Remoteness: Not more than two-to-three hours driving time, but remote enough where weapons fire (for training purposes) will not alarm anyone. If forced to "bug out," in the middle of, or on the other side of a societal collapse, you are just asking for trouble, in the form of roadblocks, ambushes, hostile areas, etc. Therefore, you want to spend as little time on the road, as possible (this of course does not refer to the people who have already bugged out, and are already living on their own rural property, having responded early to the current economic decline).

- The ability to grow food. Notice I didn't say farming or gardening. There can be many options here (unattended planting, food forest, permaculture, etc.). Make sure that the area has good sunlight exposure from the south during the growing season (remember: The Sun will be higher in the horizon), and decent soil. If there is a tendency for people to come through the area, then try to plant only below-ground crops (potatoes, garlic, etc.). There will be more on this, and the building-up of soil later in this book.

b. How to Live Well in the Current Economic Environment

Way before I was ever a peak oiler, or a full-blown survivalist, I have always been intrigued by the *Voluntary Simplicity* movement. These are people who, even during very good economic periods, have decided that more money was not adding any more quality to their lives. This movement originally started in Seattle, Washington, and spread like wildfire throughout the US. Books like *Your Money or Your Life*, by Vicki Robin and Joe Dominguez have been best-sellers.

The best sources of information on economic self-reliance are not the mainstream media. Of course, there are *some* good sources for personal financial info in the mainstream media, such as Dave Ramsey, Clark Howard, and a few others. Other mainstream, advisors, like Suze Ormon, in particular, have corporate backers, who really *don't* want to empower people financially, and are clearly constructs of *The Matrix* (Ormon's latest notoriety is her "Suze Ormon Debit Card," which from what I understand, is full of hidden fees). These people are constantly telling people how to "improve their credit score," and not even mentioning the idea of getting out of all debt, *period*. Personally, I do not want to spend the rest of my life trying to fulfill some "score."

This is one of the main reasons why I love the "underground" publishing community. These are the publishers, such as *Paladin Press*, *Eden Press*, *Delta Press*, etc. These are the most empowering libraries of "how to" information I have ever come across. While these publishers have reputations for books on weapons, re-printed military field manuals (FM's), survival, privacy (and just overall using the system to your advantage), etc., they also have some of the best books on financial independence that I've ever seen. Using the allegory of *The Matrix* once again, these publishers were putting out books before many of us (including myself) were even aware of The Matrix's existence!

Two of my favorite books on financial self-reliance are *Living Well on Practically Nothing: Revised Edition* by Ed Romney (Deceased, and not related to any politician), and *Ragnar's Guide to the Underground Economy*, by Ragnar Benson. Benson is a noted survival expert, and for decades, has written extensively for Paladin Press.

In *Living Well on Practically Nothing*, parts of Ed Romney's book are virtually comical, as he describes "A Day of Cheap Living" (Ch. 2):

> ...I awaken to the sound of a battery-powered alarm clock I bought in a flea market. It is not digital and does not have to be programmed. I hate digital things...My wife made my short-sleeved shirt from a long-sleeved worn-out dress shirt that I used to wear at weddings and funerals.
>
> My watch is a cheap Timex. My wallet is from a flea market and cost a dollar. Shoes are either generic athletic sneakers bought in the flea market or expensive Florsheim dress shoes bought in 1990 and now twice resoled and too scuffed to wear to church.

I shower with low-cost, natural gas-heated hot water. The shower nozzle is specially made to conserve water. Sometimes I get clean by swimming in the lake with a cake of soap instead and we can turn off the hot-water heater. I shave with flea-market blades *(Ouch!)* – about three cents each – or an old second-hand razor. I use ordinary soap instead of shaving cream. I now use toothpaste but I have often brushed with table salt instead and I am known to use ordinary white string for dental floss.

An attic fan made from a $15 Kmart room fan and run in the morning to save air conditioning cools the house...

I think you get the idea here. Some of Romney's other chapters are entitled, "Some Ways to Live on No Money at All" (caretaking, house-sitting, living off the land, etc.), and "Mobile Shelter" (living out of pickup trucks, vans, camper trailers, etc.). As the latest edition of this book is copyright dated 2001, a few aspects of this book are outdated: Primarily his suggestions on which automobiles to own. However, the rest of the information in this book is virtually timeless.

Ragnar's Guide to the Underground Economy is a relatively small book, measuring at only 8 ½ x 5 ¾ and 174 pages, but is full of detailed, how-to information. Although I have never worked in this capacity, Benson goes into detail describing why someone would want to work off-grid, and describes various career fields in detail, to include everything from personal gardening, to making a living as a self-employed lumberjack, caretaker, mechanic, locksmith, working in tree removal, etc.

If I can add anything from my own insight to the previously mentioned sources of economic empowerment in this chapter, it would be one that I discovered, based on my other priority as a survivalist: Physical fitness.

There are various nation-wide fitness center chains, such as *LA Fitness*, *24-Hour Fitness*, etc. I have discovered that for about $30.00 a month, you can have unlimited access to these facilities, to include their shower and locker room facilities. In other words, living out of a pickup truck, van, etc. has never been easier! You now have unlimited access to shower facilities, throughout the US! A national-chain fitness center membership, especially while living on the road, is not a bad deal. Besides, you can actually use the rest of these fitness centers to get yourself ready for the day when you may need to run long distances, lift heavy loads, etc.

In addition, with the profusion of wi-fi hotspots, the internet and IP phoning (such as Skype), it is more convenient than ever to live off of the grid, or if down on your luck (or by choice), living out of your vehicle. It actually all seems to make sense, as the United States heads down the road to second-world status and the divide between rich and poor appears to widen.

As we continue going down the slippery slope of long-term societal decline, I also strongly recommend that adults reading this book not bring anymore children into this world. Unless you are independently wealthy, I see no reason to induce needless suffering on yourself, or others yet to be born, by bringing more children into this world, and forcing them to experience it, particularly as we deal with 1930's Depression-era levels of unemployment, rising college tuition, continuing resource scarcity, etc. We are not just looking at a decade-long depression. If you do bring children into this world, understand that they need to learn food growing skills, weapons and self-defense skills, and overall self-reliance skills, in addition to any conventional careers.

III   Alternative Energy

As survivalists, we should not be thinking about fuel-run generators and stored fuel. At least not initially. As a rule, ideally and fundamentally, we want to prepare for the worst-case scenario, which is multi-generational collapse: No fossil fuels, and no outside electricity. From this mindset, we can build-up from a solid foundation, as our finances permit. If you do have the money for hundreds of gallons of stored fuel and a generator, there is nothing wrong with this for shorter-term scenarios. However, we're preparing for total societal collapse here, *so that any other disaster that comes our way is easy.*

Sure, the "Joe Sixpack" newly introduced to preparedness will think "Yeah, I'll get prepared. I'll buy a generator, and some fuel to go with it." Again, for the worst-case scenario, this clown's five gallon fuel container will run-out, and his generator will become worthless (except maybe to someone smarter, who has their game on, in the area of engines and alternative fuels). And needless to say, he'll probably be the victim of "all the above": The envy of nosy neighbors, people wanting to come over to share the wealth, etc. Particularly in light of even recent hurricanes, such as Hurricanes Sandy and Ivan.

As Jim Rawles once mentioned in a 2012 interview with Alex Jones, in the die-off that he perceives happening in this country in the event of a grid-down collapse, there is going to be only one group of survivors: Those with wood stoves. Notice that I didn't say pellet stoves.

Pellet stoves require processed wood pellets, made from sawdust. In addition, they require electricity from a separate source, in order to run the fan that makes these stoves super-efficient. Arguably, the fan for these stoves could be run from battery-stored electricity from solar panels, a wind generator, etc. However, I can imagine using self-generated electricity for other things, besides turning a fan for a stove. Nor would I be willing to bet on my own electricity being available at any given time. More importantly, acute shortages have already occurred in the supply of wood stove pellets, even during normal times.

Good old wood stoves are awesome! Various American manufacturers are currently building newer versions of the old wood stove that are designed for multiple uses: Cooking, providing ambient heat, and water heating. Wood stoves fall into two categories: The ones designed for heating a room, and the ones designed for cooking, along with the option for heating water. The good news here is that these stoves can do a little bit of both: The giant, old-fashioned cooking stoves will definitely heat-up a room, while smaller heating stoves, like pot-belly stoves and fireplace wood stove inserts with flat tops, can at least heat food if not bake, or slow-cook, depending on the pots and pans used.

A fireplace, with wood stove insert. Notice the large, flat area directly on top. This area can be used to heat food, keep other food and drink items warm, etc.

Another ideal wood (and other biomass) fueled stove is the rocket stove. The name comes from the fact that these are so efficient, that they literally look like a rocket engine, turned upside-down. Rocket stoves consist basically of a heavily insulated cylindrical chamber. At the bottom of this chamber is the combustion area, where the fuel is placed on a tray, allowing oxygen to get underneath the sticks, leaves, etc., much like the grate in a fireplace, or woodstove. These stoves are roughly 90% efficient, in this configuration. There is even a video on YouTube showing a Peace Corps volunteer showing people in Central America how to construct one of these out of 16 red bricks. Large ones have also been constructed out of 55 gallon steel drums. To make a long story short, even a small one, like the one pictured below (from StoveTec Systems, of Eugene, Oregon) can cook meals for large groups of people, with just a small amount of sticks and twigs!

Rocket stoves also have a tactical aspect to them. If you don't want the neighbors or anyone else noticing your cooking, you can simply pick it up and position it wherever you want (as long as it is not indoors). Also, you can turn the fuel-loading opening away from anyone's view. Using the pot skirt (as shown in the image) also reduces the amount of visible light seen from the stove. And needless to say, due to their efficiency, they make very little, if any smoke.

My own rocket stove. When I first used this, I simply placed some kindling underneath the small sticks that I used for fuel, and with a single match, it was as easy to light as a gas stove! With a grill pan, I was cooking up Ribeye steaks in no time!

Indoor Lighting

For indoor lighting, make sure to save all those old candles! As survivalists, we should always have them in our inventory, anyway (They have an indefinite storage life, after all). A lot of people like to give them away, or sell them at yard sales, etc. Just make sure to use safe candle holders that use glass enclosures. If none are available, then improvise with items from your kitchen (Bowls, pie pans, etc.). During even extended emergencies, candles usually do not emit enough light to draw anyone's attention, depending on the circumstance. In a hard, societal collapse scenario, however, we will want to maintain our light discipline, as described elsewhere in this book.

Another item that I discovered at a preparedness expo was an item called a "solar light bulb." These are shaped in the design of a regular screw-in light bulb, but are not intended to be screwed into any light socket. I think that this is so that people can readily identify their purpose (since many aid-workers bring them with to third-world countries). On one side are solar cells, a single AA-size NiMH (Nickel-Metal Hydride) battery in the middle, and a bank of four illuminating white LED's on the other side, covered by a translucent shade. Just set them outside during the day, with the solar panel side angled at the sun. Having tried mine out in the back of my truck during a five-day camping trip, I love them! With these, prepare to practice some light discipline during hard times, as these solar powered lights shine as bright as a normal electrical light bulb! Even though they are a little spendy at roughly $25.00 per bulb, they are definitely worth it!

Solar light bulb

Based on my own experience, you will actually get more performance out of these solar light bulbs by replacing the cheapo little 1000 mAh NiMH battery (lower electrical current) with a 3000 mAh NiMH AA battery.

Alternative Energy Systems

As we move up from here, we can start thinking about larger alternative energy systems. After extensive research, I've discovered that with even all the federal and state government incentives, you are still looking at at-least a decade for a full-scale, permanent solar power system for your home to pay for itself.

In addition, the first step of installing any large system such as this requires prepping the house with more insulation, etc. Passive solar for heating is good, if you live in a region that allows for this, and your house has good exposure to the sun as it travels in the southern horizon. The best examples that I have seen of this were (partial) underground homes, with windows facing south. In addition, passive solar water heaters work well, even in higher latitudes. The nation of Israel even requires all homes in that country to have a passive water heater installed.

Anything that generates a lot of heat (in other words, wattage) generally cannot be run by solar or wind, unless you have the battery storage, and a large enough electrical generating capability. You are basically limited to anything that you currently run on 120 VAC. This means that the largest appliances that you will be able to run will be your refrigerator, your clothes washer, your dish-washing machine, and everything else on-down. Unless you live in a southern state (and/or a constant high-wind area), and have a huge solar and wind array, you will not be able to run your 240 VAC appliances, such as any electrical heating, your electric oven, electric water heater, or your clothes dryer. This is what people mean when they say that these alternatives do not "scale-up," compared with fossil fuels, or large municipal power grids. People have to lower their expectations when switching to alternative energy.

My own personal choice has been the newer trend towards "solar generators." These are basically just large (and heavy) boxes with deep-cycle batteries in them, with a charge controller, and other hardware that allows you to charge the batteries from solar panels, wind, or the 120 VAC from another generator. I like these for the following reasons:

- They're portable (and therefore, tactical), meaning that we can move them inside of our house while they are in operation, in order to avoid nosy neighbors, and theft. They can be transported in the event of an actual "bug out." The solar panels are also portable, and can be set-up out-of-view from neighbors, while still angled towards the sun.

- They silently charge batteries, if the sun is out, or if there is wind, for a wind generator that is tied to it. During an emergency, we do not want to advertise the use of a fuel-run generator, with the noise they tend to make. In addition, for safety reasons, *fuel-run generators need to stay outdoors, while operating.*

- Also, if you have a friend or neighbor who *is* running a generator, you might be able to arrange for that person to provide additional charging for your system.

Mine, the "Powerhub 1800" will take a charge from three different sources: Solar panels, a wind generator, or from another 120 VAC source. In other words, if you know that a bad storm is coming, for instance, you can simply plug the unit into the wall, and completely charge the batteries, prior to the event. With enough 12 VDC deep-cycle batteries, you can provide power for everything in the house, other than the 240 VAC appliances previously mentioned ("1800" refers to the amount of wattage that this particular system can handle). This is provided that you can maintain a charge in the batteries with solar panels, or a wind generator. This particular system can also do "grid tie-in," meaning you can hook it up directly to your house's incoming municipal panel, for a more permanent set-up. Talk about versatile! However, you need to make sure that the breakers are turned-off for the higher wattage devices previously mentioned.

Again, as mentioned in Chapter One, we can't run our current industrialized civilization on wind and solar. This isn't meant to discourage anyone, on a personal level. Many people out there are generating surplus amounts of their own energy, and have an abundance for their own needs. It just requires an investment in dollars, planning, education, and possible lifestyle change. In my case, I actually enjoy getting up in the morning from under a pile of blankets to a cold house, then getting the wood stove going, making some coffee, and enjoying the wood stove with my little feline daughter (my cat).

IV   Food and Water Before, During and After a Societal Collapse

a. Water

The only thing more important than staying hydrated is breathing.

The American Red Cross recommends 1 gallon per person per day. They recommend that you have three days supply of water in case you need to evacuate your home, and two weeks supply at your home. Store the water out of direct sunlight and away from chemicals. The following information is presented in a dry, bulleted format, only because drinkable water is simply the most important aspect of this chapter.

Water that is safe to drink:

• Bottled water

• Melted ice cubes

• Water drained from an undamaged hot water heater

Water that needs to be treated before drinking:

• Water from the faucet that looks cloudy

• Water from a stream, creek, pond, or lake

• Rainwater

Unsafe sources of water:

• According to the American Red Cross and FEMA, water is not safe to drink from radiators, waterbeds, or swimming pools (However, water can be distilled from these and other sources through distillation).

• According to FEMA, water in toilet tanks and the bowls is unsafe. However, this water can still be used for washing, cleaning, etc., especially if detergents or bleach are used.

• According to the US Department of Homeland Security (DHS), since floodwater usually contains toxic chemicals, it cannot be purified. *Never* try to purify or use floodwater (I hate to use this federal department as a source, but they are not lying). If you are unsure of the quality of your water, purify it before using. According to the DHS website: "...water from questionable sources may be contaminated by a variety of microorganisms, including, bacteria and parasites that cause diseases such as dysentery, cholera, typhoid, and hepatitis. All water of uncertain purity should be treated before use.

The American Red Cross recommends using the following six steps to treat water:

1. Filter the water using a piece of cloth or coffee filter to remove solid particles.

2. Bring it to a rolling boil for at least 1 full minute.

3. Let it cool at least 30 minutes – water must be cool or the chlorine treatment below will not work.

4. Chlorinate: Add 16 drops (1/8 teaspoon) of liquid chlorine bleach per gallon of water (8 drops per 2-liter bottle). Stir to mix. Sodium hypochlorite (concentration of 5.25% to 6%) should be the only active ingredient in the bleach. There should not be any added soap or fragrance. According to DHS, a major bleach manufacturer has also added Sodium Hydroxide as an active ingredient, which they state does not pose a health risk for water

treatment.

5. Let stand 30 minutes.

6. If the water has *a slight* smell of chlorine, you can use it. If it does not smell of chlorine, repeat steps 4 and 5 above. If it smells of chlorine after the second try, you can use it. Otherwise, discard it and find another source of water. Remember: Chlorine is a carcinogen, so we do not want to use more than absolutely necessary.

A rainwater catchment barrel, made from a blue food-storage barrel, window screen, bungee cord, PVC-pipe valve, and large aquarium fittings. This design also has a relief outlet that feeds back into the downspout (next)

Angled downspout fitting, and overflow outlet opening that feeds excess water back into the downspout. I highly recommend a large outlet for more flow, during torrential rains.

Other good methods for treating water:

• Water Purification Tablets

• Water filters, such as the British Berkfeld ("Big Berkey") system, Katadyn Pocket Microfilter, or other small, personal suction / gravity operated filter systems.

b. Food Storage

There are many misconceptions about stored food, and how to store it. Fortunately, thanks to the internet, there is a lot of information from the agricultural departments of various universities, where lab work has been done on canned foods that have been stored for decades, in often less-than-ideal conditions. Also, there is currently an explosion of information available that shows people how to preserve and store their own food. Unfortunately, there is also a lot of market propaganda, telling people that they have to purchase freeze-dried foods and MRE's, in order to have a serious stored food supply.

If you are just now jumping onto the survival / preparedness bandwagon, and you can afford it, then sure, go out and spend nearly $200 dollars on a six-pack case of #10 cans of freeze-dried vegetables, stored in nitrogen, that will last the next 30 years (I personally think that food stored in this manner will store a lot longer than that, but the industry has to put a numerical time-figure on it, for sales purposes). I have purchased flavored TVP (textured vegetable protein), canned cheese, and butter from emergency food suppliers, to form a quickly put-together "core" of my own stored food. I then began stocking other basic items, such as rice (*white* rice, *never* brown rice. Brown rice does not last as long in storage, due to the inherent oils, and also takes considerably more time and energy to cook, whereas white rice only needs to soak, in extreme cases, making it the "queen" of stored survival foods), flour, dry goods bought in bulk, powdered milk (there are different ways to mix powdered milk, where it doesn't *taste* like powdered milk), canned food, etc.

I'd like to begin here with a discussion on the military's Meals Ready to Eat, more commonly known as MRE's, the military's replacement for the C-Ration meals, beginning in the early 1980's. Everybody currently jumping onto the preparedness bandwagon thinks that they need to store cases (12 MRE's per) of these. They're ideal for what they were intended for: Pre-packaged, self-contained meals for high-intensity combat and training environments, where you can heat the main course in a chemical water-activated heater, or eat cold. The entire MRE meal fits in a standard military-sized cargo pocket. They can be eaten, and even heated in a cargo pocket, while on the move. Almost every single food item in an MRE is fortified with extra vitamins and minerals.

However, let's look at the disadvantages of MRE's for preppers and survivalists:

• Too much packaging: sealed packages, inside of cardboard boxes, inside of sealed packages, which take up way too much space, for the limited amount of food (in my opinion) held within an MRE. Although not very heavy, MRE's can take up a lot of space, within a backpack, or in cases stored on shelves in your doomstead, when we may already be dealing with limited shelf space. Also, all that extra packaging creates a waste disposal issue. However, some of the waste can be re-utilized: The plastic MRE case can be used as an improvised canteen, the cardboard boxes can be used as fire starters, etc.

• Too much candy: We don't need sugar in a survival situation, except for flavored drinks, etc (nothing wrong with occasional "comfort foods," however). I always felt the candy was intended for appeal to the younger troops, along with the tradition of GI's handing candy out to the kids, for the "hearts and minds" effect, during wartime / foreign occupation. Not that there is any problem with candy and deserts during off-time, or down-time periods.

• Limited shelf life: Typically, MRE's are only considered usable for about a decade after they leave the factory. However, I suspect, as with most other types of long-storage foods that the flavor and nutritional content will probably last much longer, depending on storage conditions.

• Too many redundant accessories: Matches, toilet paper, bottles of Tabasco, sugar, tea, coffee creamer, etc. However, one could take apart several MRE meals, and repack the separate items, to so as to take up less space; based on individual needs (this is very common in the military). You should already have these items on hand, and organized separately. Remember, as survivalists, we may utilize military resources (skills and equipment), but we have to train and logistically plan differently than the military does. After all, the military usually has endless re-supply. We don't.

I would personally rather utilize shelf space with canned food, consisting of whole meals in a can: Canned foods such as chili and ready to eat soups, along with canned spaghetti, ravioli, etc. Canned fruits and vegetables are good ideas as well, but you want to focus on protein and calories. You will get much more caloric content out of a typical store-bought 86-cent can of chili, than an MRE main course. I'm not trying to totally dissuade people from having some MRE's in their larder. As in the military application for MRE's, they can serve the survivalist well while traveling for any reason, such as performing long-range walking patrols of the area around their home, or while traveling by vehicle post-collapse, in order to rescue family members from a distant location, etc.

Good old canned food is my favorite form of food storage, for a number of reasons:

- It's everywhere, and the average person new to prepping can instantly begin building-up a larder.
- The shelf-life of canned food is *actually much longer* than what we are usually told, or what is printed on the cans themselves.

The following is from the archives of the FDA, originally published in *FDA Consumer* magazine, regarding canned food recovered from the Steamboat *SS Bertrand*, which sank in 1865:

> The Canning Process:
> Old Preservation Technique Goes Modern
> by Dale Blumenthal
>
> The steamboat Bertrand was heavily laden with provisions when it set out on the Missouri River in 1865, destined for the gold mining camps in Fort Benton, Mont. The boat snagged and swamped under the weight, sinking to the bottom of the river. It was found a century later, under 30 feet of silt a little north of Omaha, Neb.

Among the canned food items retrieved from the Bertrand in 1968 were brandied peaches, oysters, plum tomatoes, honey, and mixed vegetables. In 1974, chemists at the National Food Processors Association (NFPA) analyzed the products for bacterial contamination and nutrient value. Although the food had lost its fresh smell and appearance, the NFPA chemists detected no microbial growth and determined that the foods were as safe to eat as they had been when canned more than 100 years earlier.

The nutrient values varied depending upon the product and nutrient. NFPA chemists Janet Dudek and Edgar Elkins report that significant amounts of vitamins C and A were lost. But protein levels remained high, and all calcium values "were comparable to today's products."

NFPA chemists also analyzed a 40-year-old can of corn found in the basement of a home in California. Again, the canning process had kept the corn safe from contaminants and from much nutrient loss. In addition, Dudek says, the kernels looked and smelled like recently canned corn.

I think you get the idea. 100 years later, and the food was still safe to eat, after simply losing some nutritive content!

Another more recent example comes from a BBC story about some 67 year-old lard:

German pensioner eats 64-year-old US lard

A German pensioner who received a tin of American lard 64 years ago in an aid package has only just tasted it, after discovering that it is still edible.

"I just didn't want to throw it away," said Hans Feldmeier, 87.

Food safety experts in Rostock, his home town on Germany's Baltic coast, said the pig fat was still safe to eat.

Mr. Feldmeier was a student in 1948 when the US was running a huge aid programme to rebuild war-ravaged Germany. He kept the tin of lard for emergencies.

A retired pharmacist, he decided to get the lard tested because of the debate about expiry dates and food safety.

A food expert, Frerk Feldhusen, said the lard was rather gritty and tasteless and hard to dissolve, though quite edible. Mr. Feldmeier provided some black bread to go with it.

The red, white and blue tin of Swift's Bland Lard bore no expiry date.

Mr. Feldhusen said the test result might make some consumers think twice before discarding food immediately after the expiry date.

As with any commercial industry, there are some misconceptions about stored food that are propagandized by the freeze-dried emergency food industry. Many businesses claim that the only way to store food for 20-30 years is to have it freeze-dried, in #10 cans, which also have the oxygen purged out of them, and in some cases, replaced with nitrogen. They say this, mainly because the freeze-drying process can only be done commercially, and not in the home.

Creating a vacuum, then replacing the oxygen with nitrogen has been a common practice in aerospace and military applications for decades, as a way to preserve sensitive electronics, for everything from space probes to military night vision devices. A key item to remember is that oxygen is a corrosive, and nitrogen is a preservative.

Using this logic, and you happen to be a beer drinker, good news! If you like Guinness Draft, in particular (which was not even available in bottles until relatively recently), then stock up! All other conventional beers that are brewed with CO_2 age after several months. Guinness, and other nitrogen-brewed beers should keep (theoretically, at least) forever. In addition, having drunk Guinness Draft in Ireland, I can vouch for the fact that there is no difference between what is brewed and bottled in Ireland, or in the US.

Canning and vacuum sealing of dehydrated goods are different, however. Both canning and vacuum sealing can be done at home, and are the primary components of food preservation. In my case, I have been preserving my own garden-grown produce for some time, from a system I developed that starts with dehydrating, then vacuum-sealing, using ordinary mason jars.

Vacuum sealing using mason jars is not just for the dehydrated stuff from your garden. My favorite section of the local Winco grocery outlet is the bulk dry goods section, where everything from pancake mix, to herbs, spices, and even candy are stored in bulk. I regularly buy items like dehydrated onion flakes, parmesan cheese, croutons, etc., take them home, transfer them to mason jars, then vacuum seal them. Even though we regularly use these items, we still vacuum seal them in order to retain all of the freshness of these dry goods. We primarily do this in order to continue our transitioning process, as we prepare for conceivably hard times ahead. In other words, while other people will be literally eating each other (due to a given scenario) years after an event, our house will still be using fresh croutons, parmesan cheese, etc.

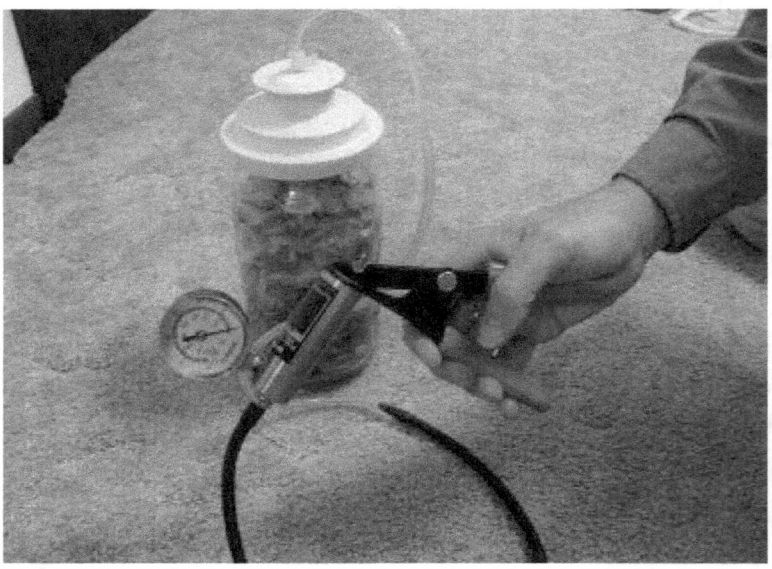

Dehydrated Yukon Gold potatoes (garden grown) being vacuum-sealed inside of a mason jar, using a Tilia-brand Mason jar adaptor and a Harbor Freight-brand brake bleeding tool. Dehydrating, then vacuum sealing your own food allows you to grow, and then preserve your own 20-30 year shelf-life foods.

Overall, we can conclude that like with any other industry based on a popularly perceived demand, the preparedness movement is no exception. The whole #10 can dehydrated food industry is trying to convince every Johnny Punchclock and Wendy Winecooler that in order to become preppers, they need to buy freeze-dried, nitrogen-packed food, in order to survive a disaster. While food packaged in this manner has its uses, this is simply not true for the individual prepper or survivalist. Besides, not everyone wants to spend nearly $200.00 per six-can case of green beans. However, Wal-Mart now sells dehydrated and vacuum sealed (not nitrogen-packed), preparedness food items. If you can afford it, I highly recommend building-up a "core" of dehydrated, #10 can products such as whole egg, cheese powder, butter powder, powdered milk, etc. If you're a family on a budget, try to buy at least one #10 can, or sealed bucket of rice, wheat, etc each shopping trip. Just think: If worst-comes-to-worst, your family will still be having scrambled eggs and potatoes breakfasts, while your neighbors (if any are left) will be fighting over the last few grains of uncooked rice.

Save your clear plastic two-liter pop bottles! By cutting the top off with something very sharp, you now have a multi-use funnel, with a threaded cap!

c. Gardening

While I am not a certified expert on organic gardening, or permaculture (I have a lot of friends who are, at least), I do have a few years of experience growing my own food. Gardening really is a joyful experience in itself, whether you are a prepper, or not. Going out into the dirt, and forming a relationship with everything living out there *really is* the way us human beings were meant to live. And again (without being too repetitive here), we wonder why successive societies, empires, and civilizations throughout the last 10,000 years have collapsed.

Tomato seedlings started indoors, germinated from saved seed. The soil used is from mature, home-made compost, with a simple fluorescent shop light used as an artificial grow light. Other than the electricity for the light (which could easily come from an alternative source), there were no outside inputs to this process.

First of all, we want to stick with organic gardening for two main reasons:

- We would otherwise have to take up valuable storage space in order to stockpile chemical fertilizers. In addition, we may have to use said space to store certain pesticides, such as snail and slug bait. Having bugs and other pests eating out of our potential survival garden is not an option.

- Chemical fertilizers kill the natural biota in the soil, thereby making your crops dependant on the artificial fertilizer. This is analogous to a drug addict needing his fix. Most industrialized agriculture today consists of monocroos (primarily corn, in the continental US) using dead soil as a sponge, where fossil fuel-based fertilizers and pesticides are sprayed on it, in order to grow food (hence, the main reason why we are losing topsoil, globally).

The result of growing tomatoes organically. The largest tomato shown measured-in at almost six inches in diameter (next photo). Not only was the size on par with commercially-grown tomatoes, but these were also the best tomatoes that I have ever tasted.

I have discovered on my own that gardening can be very simplified, compared to a lot of the information we are given: "Oh, you have to take samples of your soil, and get it tested," or "you have to lay down cardboard, or old carpet, in order to kill the lawn / weeds, then pay someone to haul a truckload of manure out to your property, to spread on top of it." Granted, everyone's soil quality is different, and if you have the time, and the money, sure, you can throw money at it, and go heavy duty all at once. I don't have any issue with that. At the time of this writing, I do have a particular sense of urgency, and if people have more money right now than they have skills, I say go for it.

As I emphasize in other areas of this book, preparedness and self reliance should be more of a lifestyle, anyway, rather than "Oh shit, this, and this, is coming, and this is what we need to get done, and I need to bust my ass."

We'll begin with first things first: Your soil. Some of us are blessed to live in areas of the country with good soil fertility. Others may have mostly clay or simply hard, dead dirt around their house. Regardless, we all need to perform this first, most important step: Composting! And I mean start composting, as of *yesterday*.

All composting is, is taking your yard debris (instead of paying the city to haul it away with your garbage), along with most other organic waste from your kitchen, along with shredded paper, wood ashes, etc, and mixing it together, and leaving it to sit on the ground, to decompose. The worms, already in the soil (hopefully) start eating the decomposing material, and leave their waste. Worm doo-doo, or worm castings, as they are formally called, are the most potent form of organic fertilizer.

After a few months, and going out there in your yard to turn the pile once in a while, bingo: You just added fresh, living topsoil to your yard! Although I am not an expert on the subject, the global loss of thousands of tons of topsoil each year is another sub-crisis, facing our civilization (as it has many previous ones). Many place the depletion of topsoil at number two, next to the worldwide depletion of crude oil reserves (and for good reason, because of the relationship between fossil fuel-based fertilizers and modern industrialized agriculture).

The table on the following page shows sources of carbon, nitrogen and composting organisms. This will give you a good idea of the things that you can put into a compost pile:

High Carbon "Browns"	High Nitrogen "Greens"	Sources of Composting Organisms
Leaves	Grass	Old Compost
Dead Plants	Green Weeds	Soil
Straw	Manure	Cow Manure
Shredded Paper	Alfalfa or Clover	Chicken Manure
Shredded Twigs	Seaweed or Pond Algae	Horse Manure
Pine Needles	Non-Meat and Non-Dairy Kitchen Scraps	Commercially Available Composting "Starters"
Sawdust from Untreated Wood		Old Compost

Source: The Basics of Home Composting: Guide to Home Composting, State of Pennsylvania: www.pa.gov

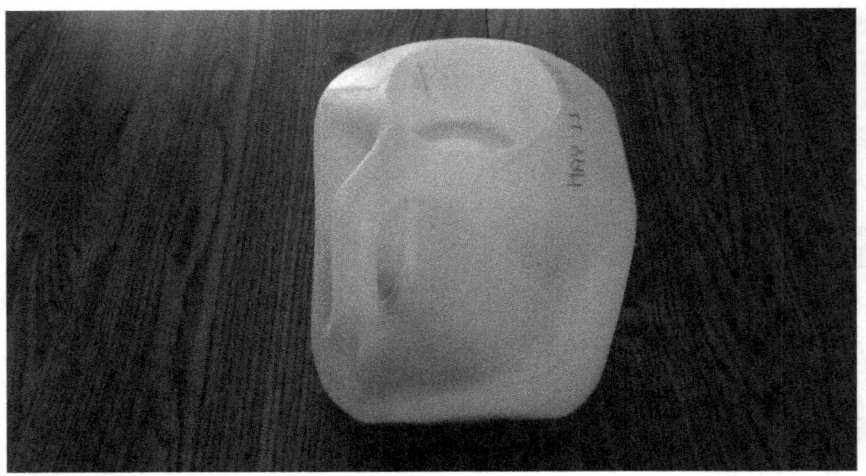

This is a compost bucket made from a one-gallon milk jug, with built-in handle. Simply cut a wider hole in the top of the jug, and you can keep it handy in your kitchen, to dump food waste, coffee and coffee grounds, used paper tissues, dryer lint, etc. Homemade compost tends to be richer than commercial compost, based on the wider variety of inputs. Used milk jugs also come in handy in the garden as watering containers, in order to transfer water from your rain barrels to your garden.

From various sources, and my own experience, I do not use wooden boxes, or fancy mixers, that resemble small cement mixers. I simply start a pile after mowing the lawn, or pulling a bunch of weeds, etc. I put this pile directly on the ground, on or near an area where I plan to plant a crop. This brings the worms up into the compost pile from underground, which also enriches the existing soil underneath. It also kills any grass and weeds under the pile (you don't need cardboard, or any other outside material to kill unwanted plants in a planting area). Also, I do not pay attention to ratios of carbon or nitrogen. However, for proper decomposition, try to make sure that the material that you put into a compost pile is no larger than your little finger.

One thing that is not mentioned in the preceding chart is urine. Urea is a powerful organic fertilizer, from any source, including humans. As a matter of fact, dried urea is even a tradeable commodity among farmers in various countries. It has even been theorized that a person's own urine can provide the entire nutrient necessary to grow food for that person. You can just go outside and piss on your newest compost pile, or piss in a container, then dump the urine on the pile. Needless to say, urine will actually speed-up the decomposition process in compost piles.

Although I have been warned not to do this, I have had no problems applying urine directly to the base of an above-ground producing plant (not below-ground crops like potatoes, garlic, etc). We must remember: Organic fertilizers work slowly, just as one would take protein as part of a physical training program. Chemical fertilizers work fast, as if said athlete were taking steroids, which produces good appearance, and bad side effects (such as produce with less taste, "dead" soil, etc).

Many sources on the subject of composting warn against adding any meat, dairy products, bones, or manure from certain animals. However, more organic farmers are coming out of the woodwork to challenge some of this philosophy.

Small amounts of meat are not going to hurt anything in a compost pile (such as uneaten pet food, etc). As for dairy products, I don't see the problem, since any organisms inherent are probably more on the probiotics side: The bugs that are already in our gut that contribute to our digestive and immune systems.

Here are the things that you *do not* want to throw into a compost pile:

- Human Waste: The pathogens in human feces are an outright biohazard, and the disease effects are lethal. There *is* a process known as *humanure*, or composting with human feces. However, this requires the use of a specific compost medium for the feces, which is usually sawdust. Also, you have to monitor the temperature of what's in the bathroom bucket, with a meat thermometer. You have to achieve certain temperatures for proper decomposition. To make a long story short, it's complex, time consuming, and if you don't do everything right, you end up with a compost pile contaminated with pathogens. Certain Scandinavian countries have developed large-scale residential systems for recovering human waste to be used for composting, but these systems are not legal in the US, and are beyond the practical scope of this book. Until recent times, the Chinese exclusively used human waste directly on crops, as fertilizer. This is also the reason why until recently that the Chinese never ate raw, fresh vegetables: They always stir-fried them as a basic rule, within their culture.

- Bones: As we all know, they don't decompose, so don't use them.
- Manure from meat-eating animals (cats, dogs, us, etc). Manure from any *non-meat-eating* animal (cows, chickens, horses, etc) is OK.

Make separate compost piles every time you mow the lawn, pull weeds, dump a large pile of shredded paper on the ground, etc. After a while, you will notice some of your piles appearing to be at the same stage of decomposition. At this time, you can go ahead and combine these piles that have caught-up to each other in the decomposing process. Never continue adding new material to a several weeks-old compost pile (unless it's the only / newest one you have, and you're adding small amounts of kitchen scraps, etc.). All you are doing is delaying the composting process. The best tools for moving and turning compost piles are the small, short-handled pitchforks that you can buy at the big-box hardware stores.

When your piles shrink, and they look like just another small (or large, from combining them) pile of rich soil, presto! You now have fresh, virgin topsoil! Also, homemade compost is even richer than commercial compost, because of the broader variety of stuff that you threw in: Everything from coffee grounds, to shredded paper, to urine.

Obviously, there is more to producing your own food than what can realistically be added to this book. I focused primarily on

Three separate compost piles, at different levels of decomposition. The one on the far left is mostly leaves, which take longer to decompose. The other two were close to the same level of decomposition, and were later combined.

composting here because of the urgent need to begin building topsoil, at both the micro, and macro levels. I highly recommend building a hard-reference library on gardening. Vegetable gardening how-to books can be found very cheap at thrift stores, yard and garage sales, etc. Particularly good books worth buying are *Gardening When it Counts* by Steve Solomon, or the late Carla Emory's *The Encyclopedia of Country Living*.

Get kids started early in gardening. They love it! This little two year-old actually got excited every time he was around compost piles! This is crucial, as the younger generations, starting with the present generation of 20-somethings are being left with nothing but the table scraps (bleak economic outlook, global fiat currency collapse, resource depletion and climate change) of our current industrialized civilization.

d.   Foraging

Foraging is basically just identifying the edible stuff that grows naturally in your location, and going out to get it. Try getting one of those folding, laminated guides to edible plants here in North America. Once you learn what is edible in your area, you will begin to realize that we are literally walking on top of food (yes, even the grass growing in your front yard is edible).

I suggest seeking out any meet-up (awareness) groups in your local area, such as peak oil, or permaculture groups that meet-up at least once a month. Many of these groups hold book readings, and bring in subject-matter-expert guest speakers, who discuss things related to gardening, foraging for wild edibles, etc. Some of these groups may seem really hippie-dippy, or senior citizen (or both), but many of these people represent the opposite-end of the collapse / doomer spectrum: The eco-hippie doomers, who are big on intellect. They know all about peak oil theory, the 1972 *Limits to Growth* study, etc., but *most of them* are short on any real, practical skills, to include firearms, in particular.

Hopefully this chapter was able to provide a general overview, while providing some big takeaways. For instance, many of the details regarding food preservation and storage are beyond the scope of this book. These takeaways are based on my own personal experience, and my households' current transitioning.

V. Nutrition

While I am not a nutritional expert, I can vouch for the things that I have experience with, within my own diet. This will be a short chapter, as I will only cover a couple of items that I have personally had experience with, within recent years: Mainly probiotics, and the elimination of salt from my diet. It is pointless for me to write some descriptive piece about the perfect diet, and expect the reading public to have the self-discipline to stick to it. Even I am not that self-disciplined.

Probiotics refer to the "good" bacteria that exist in our intestinal tract, that help us process waste. Foods that contain these good live bacteria (more commonly referred to commercially as "active cultures") are yogurt, home-made and true organic versions of sauerkraut, coleslaw, kimchi, etc. Be careful of store brands that refer to any of these products as "organic." The label will also usually state that the item was pasteurized, at a high temperature. That kills all of the live culture, and the reason for even eating the product!

I first learned about probiotics from a reference to primitive peoples eating fermented and lacto-fermented foods from Charles Eisenstein's *The Ascent of Humanity*. In that book, he brought attention to the work of the 1920's American dentist and nutritional researcher Dr. Weston A. Price. After Price had suspected that the dental problems that he was seeing in patients (in addition to non-dental medical issues that had previously been rare) had something to do with their diet of modern, processed food (even back then!), he traveled around the world, visiting primitive societies in remote locations, from the outer islands of Scotland, to Africa, and to remote islands in the Pacific Ocean. In all of the primitive cultures (by our current standards) that Price had visited and lived with:

...he found almost no tooth decay, no obesity, no heart disease, and no cancer. Instead he observed magnificent physical stamina, easy child-birth, and broad jaws with all 32 teeth. The diets were different everywhere, but there were some things in common. People ate very few refined carbohydrates, plenty of live fermented food, and substantial quantities of fats and organ meats. Their vitamin intake was many times greater than the norm today. Price's work lends support to the contention that at least in some respects, primitive people enjoyed better health than is the norm today, even without the modern medicine that we *think* keeps us healthy. (Eisenstein, p. 42).

After I had read *The Ascent of Humanity*, I had later listened to the health and fitness expert Gary Null on his Progressive Radio Network mention a study where probiotics were tested as a cure for the common cold, in a controlled, peer-reviewed experiment. In this experiment the test subjects were given probiotics like *Lactobacillus acidophilus* and *Lactobacillus paracasei*. The results showed that 50% of the test subjects did not contract a cold, even when exposed to the virus. Apparently, at least half of the strength of our immune system comes from our intestinal gut.

When my wife and I would go to public places on the weekends, many times on Monday I would have a cold. Once I started taking acidophilus in tablet form, I simply stopped catching colds. It was amazing!

Although once in a while I still get a cold, it has been due to not taking enough probiotic, or taking an inferior brand, containing only one billion active cultures per capsule. Try to find brands of acidophilus that have two billion cultures per tablet. Better yet, add vegetables like cabbage to your garden each growing season, and make your own, naturally fermented, home-made sauerkraut and cole slaw. Dr. Gary Null recommends 12-18 billion culture each day. When I was in Libya for two months in 2011, I took two of the two-billion culture tablets each morning, and never got sick once (even in some really unsanitary conditions). In addition, the local people there actually drank soured milk, rich in Lactobacilli. It tastes horrible, but the active cultures in it make yogurt look like a joke. No vaccines, no inoculations, just probiotics, to strengthen my immune system. That was all I needed. There is no reason for people to take over-the-counter aids for things like constipation, etc., when the solution is in *what* we eat

The single biggest dietary transition I have ever made was the elimination of excess salt from my diet. I don't put any on my food, and I don't use it in my cooking, even if a recipe includes it.

It started in my 30's, when as a physical artform, I performed Irish dance, in both competition and performance. At the time, I was planning on getting back into the martial arts, but was drawn to the more intense discipline of Irish dance. It was also some of the most intensive physical training I have ever done, and as a good cross-trainer, my military physical fitness scores as a military reservist skyrocketed as a result (i.e., 13:30 two-mile run times).

During this time however, I was still a salt-pig: I would put it on my french fries, *and* my fast food burgers, etc. During these intense practice sessions, I could actually feel the salt come out of my skin, and re-form on top of it. It was the grossest feeling in the world! After having this happen twice, I made the decision to go cold turkey, and not use any more salt, period.

The results were amazing! I immediately lost five pounds, and had more energy, when I did stuff. Years after I removed excess salt from my diet, I had a routine military physical at age 43, where my heart-rate, even at rest, with no prior exercise that day, was only 40 beats per minute! They initially thought something was wrong with their equipment! This is an idea of how healthy our early ancestors really were (and how healthy we can become), despite all of the Hobbsian crap that we have always been brainwashed with within our culture, about pre-civilizational man.

I highly encourage the readers of this book to quit taking over the counter drugs that treat symptoms of things like insomnia, heartburn, constipation, etc., and find the natureropathic cures, in things like vitamins, probiotics, herbs, etc. Many of our current illnesses are a result of our modern industrialized civilization.

VI Physical Fitness

Physical fitness is another core subject within this book. Along with economic preparedness, physical fitness should be given equal priority. After all, a wealthy individual who has poor health really does not have much of anything. A relatively "poor" person who has good to excellent health (to include physical fitness) has the world at their fingertips, and therefore has the potential to achieve / explore / create virtually anything in this world that they want. My own fitness level allowed me the freedom to travel to Libya in 2011, in order to assist a very peaceful people (almost to a fault) with their backs against the wall, against one of the most brutal dictators (and exporters of terrorism) of the last 50 years.

Lack of physical fitness and obesity are the primary causes of virtually all of our other diseases, for everything from lowered immunity to cancer.

Although this subject probably deserves its own chapter, getting all of your elective surgeries and treatments done now is imperative. Anyone who has poor eyesight, dental issues, etc. needs to get this stuff taken care of, as of yesterday. The services for treating these health issues may not be around in a few years, as things continue to socio-economically degrade, or after a regional, or global cataclysmic event. So, if you want to get away from having to use eyeglasses (a priority preparedness issue, in my opinion), or want to get a certain dental issue resolved, it needs to be done *now*.

Nothing is as good a personal confidence builder than being in excellent physical shape, except maybe the additional skills of being a martial artist (particularly the more creative and improvisational ones, primarily Kung Fu, or other Chinese-inspired art forms). And by physically fit, I mean to military, or competitive athletic standards. During my entire time in Libya, I was more than willing to travel on-foot, with my belongings (in a completely foreign environment, I might add), to another country, in the event I had to escape-and-evade my way out of a situation. All of the road marching experience I had in the military came in really handy. Also, when you know you're in good shape and physically capable, you literally project an aura of confidence. I also wanted to be able to fight my way out of a situation, if I had to. As far as I can tell, no one I met ever considered taking advantage of me in any physical way.

During the writing of this book, I have been watching some of the episodes of the TV shows on National Geographic and The Discovery Channel, previously mentioned. The people profiled range from incredibly self-reliant, to outright embarrassments to the rest of the preparedness community. Across the spectrum, many of these people, to include married couples, are overweight, and appear to lack any functional level of physical fitness, in the event of an emergency, to include armed or unarmed combat, etc.

I also have little respect for these "experts" who get huge articles posted on the subject of martial arts, physical fitness and training at websites like SurvivalBlog.com, who admit that they themselves at present are mere couch potatoes. Why aren't these guys continuing to walk the walk, if they are indeed survivalists? Preparedness means being in shape *now*, not "I used to be," or "I will be." Actors like Clint Eastwood and Charlton Heston have aged like wine, because of their emphasis on physical fitness, throughout their lives.

Also, whenever I walk into that human zoo known as Wal-Mart, I am shocked by the overweight, unhealthy masses, of all ages. I often tell people that when I enter that store that it reminds me of the dystopic sci-fi movie *Freejack*, where Emilio Estevez gets zapped into the future, escapes, then hooks up with a friend who tells him while walking through a crowd, "You stick out too much. You need to blend-in. Walk with a limp, or something." Being more physically fit than everyone else around you creates an obvious and awesome advantage.

The best form of physical fitness, whether you're military, or a survivalist, prepper, etc., is running. There is a reason why every branch of the military puts its emphasis on running in its Physical Training (PT) programs:

- Running is the ultimate cross-trainer, working every muscle in your body, in addition to your cardio-vascular system.
- Overall stamina and endurance
- The ultimate cross-trainer for traveling with backpacks (running *with one* is even better), weapons, etc.
- Being a runner also means that you are capable of staying awake for longer periods of time, due to an improved cardio-vascular system, and overall endurance. This in itself is crucial during a societal event.
- In the event of physical attack, having more endurance than your adversary, in itself, can be a great equalizer.
- Is a mandatory prerequisite prior to studying any martial arts training.
- Running simply boosts your overall energy level.

At this time, if you know you are out of shape, then drop everything else, and re-prioritize your physical fitness. It doesn't cost anything, except for maybe a pair of running shoes. This is definitely one of those areas you can work on, that cost little, to no money. Start running, at least three times a week. Even if you tell other people and yourself "Oh, I can't run," bullshit. If all you can handle is five minutes at a time, then make it five minutes each day, and build-up from there.

Begin each running session with stretching exercises. These are crucial to avoiding injury, and just preparing your muscles for a workout, overall. Even if you start out being able to run for only five minutes at a time, that is OK. As you continue going out there at least three times a week, your time running, speed, distance, etc. will improve. Most importantly, make sure you include some "cool-down" activity, such as yard work, working in the garden, etc., followed by post-workout stretching. Also, make sure that you take in a protein drink, or at least eat something immediately after your workout, since most of your body's repairing and conditioning takes place within the first hour after training.

You can even kill two birds with one stone, if you need to do any shopping in the local area, run errands (literally), etc. Just warm up as usual, put on a backpack, and go! From my experience, I've discovered that it is not a good idea to run with items like milk, eggs, etc. I have been able to run with virtually everything else. One time, I even ran with a US Army-issue ALICE pack, to go pick up a mounted motorcycle tire from a shop, wheel and all. I realized when I picked it up that I couldn't fit it inside the ruck sack itself, but no problem. I was able to strap it to the outside of the pack, using the cinched exterior straps, that are designed to accommodate sleeping bags, crew-served weapons gear, etc, and use the backpack as a packboard. Talk about some good training!

It is pretty obvious here the emphasis that I place on physical fitness. Having been in physically challenging situations, to include unarmed combat, etc., this area of preparedness cannot be overemphasized. Yes, I do hold myself to a high standard. If times get bad enough, I want to be able to shoot-and-scoot like Hawkeye, himself, in *The Last of the Mohicans*. There was a reason why he, his adopted Indian father and uncle were the last of their tribe: Because they were all bad-asses!

VII. How to Repair Things, and Make Them Last

This chapter was originally inspired by the chapter "Fix Things and Make Them Last," from Ed Romney's *Living Well on Practically Nothing*. Although much of the information from that chapter is outdated (most devices we use now, from cameras to automobiles use less moving parts, and are therefore more reliable), there are some vital takeaways, along with some of Ed Romney's personality, which I find entertaining, throughout the book. I could have included this portion within the Economic Preparedness chapter, but this self-reliance-oriented information deserves a higher priority than some of the sexier aspects (weapons, camouflage, etc.) of survivalism.

Some doomers, such as Dmitry Orlov believe that we must begin transitioning by buying older (or remanufactured versions) of tools, appliances, etc. that are designed to last 30-years-plus, without planned obsolescence built into them. I have experienced planned obsolescence myself. For instance, I still have one of a working pair of Bell South brand FRS/GMRS walkie talkies that I bought over a decade ago (the working one only transmits and receives on channel 1 now). On each one, while the electronics still worked, the latch that holds the battery compartment cover in place broke on both of them, at roughly the same time (I used a piece of electrical tape to keep the battery compartment secure on each one).

However, I would like to add a variation to this theme. How about taking the cheap crap you buy from Wal-Mart, letting it break, and then repairing *it*, to make *it* last? With a little bit of engineering, it can be done.

For instance, one day I decided I needed a heavier-duty spatula, for all the cooking I like to do (especially frying). So, at Wal-Mart I bought a heavy duty-looking spatula. After a couple of months, the thick, plastic blade of the spatula became loose, then completely fell-off of the handle!

I really liked this spatula, and it seemed more convenient (and less wasteful) to repair this one, rather than shopping for another one, that actually worked. So, I broke out the *JB Weld*, and mixed some up. After I had cleaned the tip of the metal handle that inserted into the spatula blade with alcohol, I glued the spatula back together, carefully cleaning-up any excess epoxy. It's been about two years now, and I still use that spatula, frequently.

My repaired, "heavy duty" spatula. As with anything you glue together, remember these steps: 1. Clean up both parts to be glued together as much as possible, preferably with a drying solvent (i.e., alcohol), to include loose particles with a steel brush, etc. 2. Test-fit the pieces together, then (3) apply the glue or epoxy, and then join the pieces together. If possible, either clamp, or weight-down the pieces being joined together, for a stronger bond.

Metal-filled epoxy was the big takeaway from that chapter of

Ed Romney's book. The most popular brand that everyone knows and loves is JB Weld. It consists of two equal parts that require mixing: The minute particle-ground metal base, and a white-colored hardener. In *Living Well on Practically Nothing*, Romney described everything from the crankshafts on 1000-horsepower diesel engines, to the four-cylinder engine of an abandoned Mercedes being successfully repaired, between a composite of mechanical bonding and metal-filled epoxy, or non-metallic epoxy with metal filings added (the Mercedes). The dried JB Weld is so strong, that it is also referred to as "cold welding." It can even be used to add more material to an existing metal part, and machined to size, just like the metal it is attached to! I think JB Weld is one of the greatest things ever invented for the survivalist, right up there with 550 (parachute) cord and military duct tape. After first reading that book, in the event that I ever need to improvise, and make my own metal-filled epoxy, I have recovered all of my metal filings and shavings in a zip-locked bag, religiously, ever since.

Speaking of duct tape, the old joke is that "You might be a redneck if...you consider duct tape a permanent repair." However, as I've discovered, sometimes it does make a good permanent repair, if you're using the right stuff. For instance, the military uses what is commonly known as "100 mph tape." This is basically OD green-colored duct tape on steroids that is strong enough to remove the paint from walls. This particular type of tape was originally designed during WW II, as an item to re-seal ammo cans (at that particular time, it was actually called "duck tape").

Most people, however, do not need duct tape this strong. However, as survivalists, just as with our clothing, weapons, equipment, tools, etc., we want earth tone duct tape. My favorite duct tape is the "90 mph" duct tape made by the company Brigade Quartermaster. While it is not genuine 100 mph tape, it is very strong, yet very easy to tear by hand, and to work with. It comes in a variety of earth-tone colors, to include traditional Army OD green, "low IR signature" Army ACU green. and sand color (Avoid black-colored military duct tape).

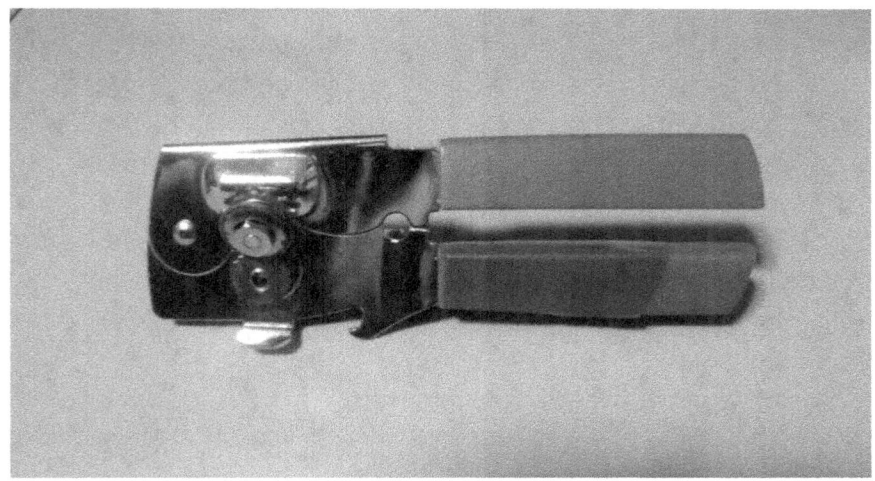

This manual can opener was originally repaired with JB Weld. However, because the plastic itself was so weak, it broke again. It was permanently repaired when I simply wrapped the broken handle with "90 mph" military-style duct tape. Yes, this is just a repair of a dumb can opener, but it is amazing how much hardship has been created in the aftermath of disasters, simply because people had no hand-operated can openers in their possession. They are the only can openers we use in our household. They're simply more convenient.

Obviously in the present, it may not be cost-effective to repair every single item, but I have discovered in my case that it is actually more convenient for me to repair something, than it is to go through the trouble of buying the same item again. In the kind of societal upheaval that most of us preppers and survivalists are ultimately preparing for, basic fabrication and repair skills are going to be a must. People who happen to be skilled auto mechanics, welders, electronics technicians, sheet metal fabricators, engineers, machinists, etc. are going to be worth their weight in gold.

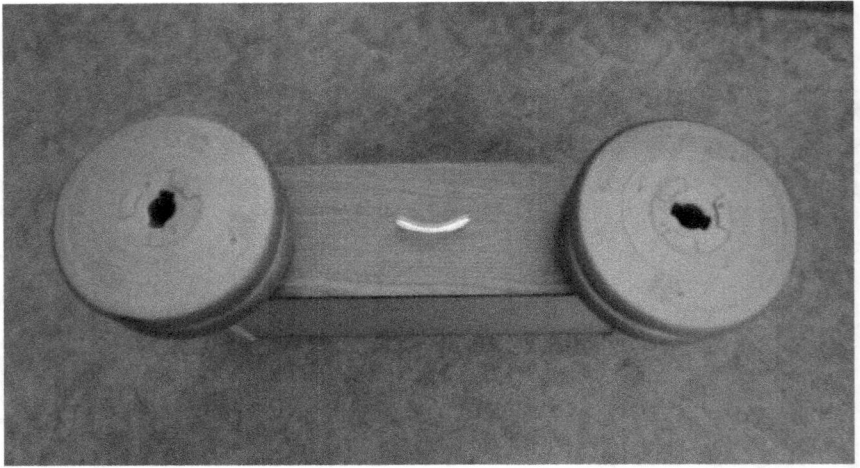

This is the top drawer from my clothes dresser. It was made of cheap particleboard to begin with, but has served me for many years. During the writing of this book, the front of the drawer came apart from the rest of the drawer, that it was simply stapled to. I cleaned-up all the loose material, test-fitted the parts, then used a common wood glue to put it all back together. In order to clamp the parts together, I used every fabricator's friend: Gravity. I simply positioned the drawer on its end and used barbell weights to clamp the parts together. Make sure you that you stand-by with a wet rag, to wipe-up any running glue, for any repairs such as this.

The following is from a sidebar piece from the chapter previously described in Romney's book *Living Well on Practically Nothing*. He describes an incredibly self-reliant family, stranded in the middle of a desert, where the father is basically on-the-spot rebuilding their truck's engine:

A MODERN PIONEER. When I was crossing the country in 1959, we camped near a giant boulder on a state road in Wyoming. A 10-year-old Dodge pickup truck was stopped there, too, with an older working man and wife and some young kids who sat in the enclosed cap on back of the truck. The man seemed to be working on the motor. After awhile we began to talk and I had a look at it. He had dropped the oil pan from the flathead six on to the ground in the shade of the big boulder in what was actually a big desert. And he was cleaning it out. He had an assortment of old insert rod bearings and he was assembling and fitting pairs of them, trying patiently to find a combination that would stop the knock in the motor from a bad rod bearing and restore oil pressure. The old bearing had failed in the extremely hot weather. None of his family, even his kids, were frightened although this was a serious problem that would certainly destroy the crankshaft and leave them stranded without transportation in the middle of nowhere if he could not fix it. They seemed to have full confidence in him. The family amused themselves, the wife read or sewed, and the kids played nicely while the father worked on the old truck. I asked him if he needed tools, which I carried, or water or oil, or my help, or if he wanted me to get help at the next town. He declined all of my offers politely. I waited to leave until he drove off with the old truck, now running fairly quietly, going in the opposite direction. I always remembered that man and his family. *That was the spirit of the pioneers alive today that I had witnessed*. Look for it yourself, encourage it. Be like that.

I agree with Romney. We had better get like that, if we are going to survive even *gradual* socio-economic decline. Most people currently in Umerican society are unable to live like this. Just one more reason why I expect a human die-off to commence this century, with people like the ones described in the preceding quote surviving through the "bottleneck."

VIII   Situational Awareness

Situational awareness is an important basic attribute, more important in-itself than any type of tactical or combative training, as it is also included, fundamentally, in these skill-sets. This is why this chapter comes before the ones on hand-to-hand combat, firearms, and surviving on a battlefield. What is the point of being highly trained in a martial art, if you didn't notice the guy in the bar, who came up behind you, and hit you with that cue stick from the pool table? Or walking down the street and you didn't notice the people walking around you in the same direction, keeping pace with you, in order to spring their ambush?

This was not an issue for me while in Libya, during the summer of 2011, being a preparedness / survivalism consultant. When walking down the street, be aware of who is not only in front of you, but also, and more importantly, who is behind you, and across the street from you. Look for people ducking into shops in front of you, or someone across the street, walking in the same direction, at the same pace. You can counter any suspected ambush by simply crossing the street, traveling in another direction, etc.

While in Libya, fortunately for me, because of the formation of the no-fly zone, and US foreign policy decisions that actually worked for once (I saw no other Americans there, in any type of official capacity from the US Government), the environment was *extremely* pro-American.

Years ago, when I served in an Army National Guard Officer Candidate program, one of the ways for the TAC (Teach, Advise, Counsel – supposedly) Officers to harass us initially was to demand that we salute them whenever we saw them from *any* distance, not just the regulation 10-feet, or so. At the time, this seemed like just one more form of abuse, on the part of a bunch of presumably educated punks, wearing uniforms. Needless to say, this was one hell of an exercise in situational awareness, of which looking back on it, was actually really good training.

One thing I have noticed recently is the need to be extremely situationally aware when confronting someone. What I mean by this is any situation where you feel morally obliged to confront someone. For example, confronting someone who is publicly abusing a child, someone who is intentionally lying about important facts to someone else in a conversation, etc. As someone once said, "Evil flourishes, because good men do nothing."

The following is a perfect example of the need for acute situational awareness in an urban environment.

At a restaurant and bar establishment, in a major city, I confronted a public figure who preaches what everyone wants to hear about societal collapse (aka "Doomer Porn"), but has not only burned many people who have previously worked for him, but has gotten himself into legal trouble repeatedly. One of these involved a sexual harassment lawsuit, which was the largest fine of its type ($200,000) in the history of the State of Oregon.

Back to the story: At the end of his public presentation, there was an after-event social at a particular establishment. Finding out about it that evening, I thought I would go to that event as well, at least to see other friends of mine there from the progressive community. While making friends with a local video producer, we both sat near this individual. While the two of us were talking, we overheard this person yelling at some new-found fans of his, a husband-and-wife pair, who wanted to talk to him. He was actually being rude to them, as he had been to virtually everyone that evening, while he was sitting there, watching this dumb collection of videos of music stage performances from the late '60's and early '70's, on a theater-sized screen. As he's yelling at them, he tells them, "I had a Q-Level security clearance when I was 11 years old!"

As a recently-retired Army Intelligence Officer, I knew this was some of the worst lying I have ever heard. I told the guy I was conversing with, "I think I need to get going. The shit's getting pretty deep around here." So, after having dinner and a beer there an hour earlier, then water to flush it all out of my system, I got up to leave. It had been a long day, as I had been working all day in my yard, while experiencing some allergic reaction after returning from Libya (which later turned out to be a developed reaction to Tea Tree Oil), and by 11 PM, was pretty tired. Also, I had not been physically training at all, with this allergic reaction all up-and-down my legs.

However, I was not going to let this go, with the star of the evening: As I was heading out, I stopped where he was sitting, and said, "So, you had a Q-Level government security clearance issued to you when you were a little kid, huh?" At that, he puts his hand up, without even looking at me, as if he's silently trying to push me away. I then told him, "That's the biggest crock of shit I've ever heard in my life." At that point, he set down his mixed drink, and just said, "Now I'm pissed." Without warning, he stood up, and grabbed the front of my shirt with both hands, and using his short stance to his advantage, pushed against me, chest-to-chest, until we both landed on the ground. As soon as it happened, his entourage pulled him off of me.

He caught me completely flat-footed! Despite all my combative knowledge, this guy attacked without the slightest warning, and I was not even in a defensive stance (otherwise I would not have been knocked off-balance, to say the least). In a more normal world, we would expect someone to respond verbally to a statement like that. Instead, this guy, a disturbed individual who cons the progressive/hippie community for a living, chose to physically assault someone, without warning. I don't think he really meant to hurt me, and likewise, myself.

This has been the sharpest lesson in urban situational awareness that I can remember. The take-away from this story:

Anyone within your immediate threat area can attack you, period, without the slightest warning. Be aware of anyone and everyone who happens to get within 10 feet of you. As we head down the long slide of societal decline, more people will be on something (legal or illegal), coming off of something, or just outright mentally disturbed.

IX   Hand-to-Hand combat and Martial Arts Training: Where to Get It

Now that we have covered physical fitness and situational awareness, we need to cover unarmed (i.e., no firearms) combat, in the contemporary environment. Remember, we're already in the beginning stages of collapse, after all. We are more likely to get into unarmed fights with someone we know, whether they're a family member, neighbor, public figure, etc (in my case, a mentally unstable con man), than we are likely to get into a shootout with someone.

In the history of the oriental martial arts, many art forms, primarily Chinese Kung Fu and Kung fu-inspired art forms (Thai Boxing, Muai Thai, Okinawan Aikido, various Philippino art forms, etc,) were created out of the need for unarmed societies to defend themselves through improvised means. At present, there seem to be metal detectors at every public event, not to mention the airports. Also, if you happen to get into a scuffle with someone and the police are later involved, you don't want to be found with a concealed weapon on your person, if it is not legal (better yet, don't consent to any searches). In addition, due to the legal implications of using a handgun outside of your home (i.e., primarily spending your life savings on lawyers), you may want to avoid carrying a handgun for self defense. I know this may sound crazy to some people, but let's look at the facts:

- Most reported violence occurs between people who actually know each other.

- According to the FBI's own statistics, violent crime has actually decreased over the years. I believe this is primarily due to the birth-dearth, since the 1960's, generating fewer younger people, relative to the Baby Boomer generation, who contributed to the crime rates of the 1960's and 70's.

- The US is currently the biggest incarcerator of people on the planet, beating even Communist China in the total number of people in prison (As Dmitry Orlov has described, the US wins "The Jails Race," in comparing the US to the Soviet Union and its gulag system, prior to its collapse). This is not to say that violent crime at the hands of strangers does not happen. Due to the early release of prisoners on fiscal grounds, we may start to see a gradual increase in violent crime (in other words, "We can't afford to house you, so we're changing the law." Talk about an indicator of a collapsing system!). However, the priority here has been with non-violent offenders, which is probably a good thing, anyway, as many of these people have been victims of decades of "get tough on crime" mandatory sentencing, etc.

I Have formally studied Korean Tae Kwon Do and Chinese Northern Shaolin Fist Style Kung Fu (a very brutal, hard artform), as well as having studied the history of the west-to-east migration of Asian martial arts. I have also studied the spread of Chinese Kung Fu, and its interpretation by other Asian nations that were influenced by it. I can conclude that the best martial artform to study is Kung Fu (and its various styles), or similar art forms that come from Okinawa (Aikido), or the Philippines (Escrima). These were heavily influenced by the spread of Chinese Kung Fu. Anything Thai is also good, such as Muy Thai (Thai boxing). The Israeli artform of Krav Maga is an even better choice, since it doesn't waste time teaching artistic form. It teaches practical techniques, courtesy of what the Israelis have experienced from their time in the Occupied Territories: The West Bank and Gaza (Not that I approve of Israeli foreign policy, since this land was taken during The 1967 War, which involved the breaking of a cease-fire, which was preceded by the intentional attack on the *USS Liberty*, an intelligence gathering vessel. And the Israelis have been taking The Holocaust out on the Palestinians, ever since).

Avoid martial arts such as Japanese Karate, Judo, and Korean Tae Kwon Do. In my opinion, these are very limited martial arts, which are big on discipline, and extremely short on creativity and improvisation. When you study Kung Fu for instance, even in the lower sashes (i.e., belts) you learn aspects of fighting that are inclusive to all of these other martial arts, that are only taught at their higher belt-levels.

For instance, while taking two years to earn a yellow sash in Northern Shaolin Fist Style, I was exposed to skills taught to me by my elder brothers and sisters that exceeded what I was being taught for my first sash. This happened during organized campouts, and at the school itself. One of the things I focused on, for instance, was *Chin Na*, also known in the western world as joint manipulation, or what law enforcement calls "control techniques." This is the sub-discipline within Kung Fu that practices controlling someone through locking tendons, inducing pain, etc. These techniques are not even taught in Japanese or Korean martial arts until you are nearly a black belt. When done effectively, *Chin Na* resembles a Jedi Master from one of the Star Wars movies, making someone submitting to them, by literally just holding their hand.

When looking for a school, the seedier, the better. Try to look for schools that place more emphasis on training adults. Some American martial arts schools try to appeal to parents with children, promising to teach respect, discipline, etc. This is a bastardization of the original intent of Chinese martial arts training, in particular. Kung Fu was originally developed to teach fighting skills and messing people-up, period. You have to understand Chinese military philosophy: That showing mercy to an enemy is seen as being cruel to yourself.

You also have to understand what the Chinese martial arts

come from: Thousands of years of non-stop warfare between warring states, and one-after-another collapsed civilizations (ever wonder why it seems like China has played the US like a cheap fiddle geopolitically since at least the French Indochina War? You simply don't have that many failed civilizations within one location, and not learn something from them).

In order to stay in business, many martial arts schools cater to children, and there is nothing wrong with this. I have come across some very good Kung Fu schools, where many children trained at. However, if the school has a more adult vibe, then you are going to learn more dirty tricks, and find good, aggressive sparing partners (I like my sparring sessions to resemble the choreography from a movie, with longer, sustained engagements, i.e., *The Matrix*, and other movies using Chinese art form). This more adult theme means that the school is not about teaching respect, or discipline, or self-confidence. It means that these schools focus on busting people-up, period.

I hope this chapter has given people an idea of where they should go for martial arts training. Remember to also find schools that are big on practical technique, and not on forms (the dance-like choreography that has to be memorized, in order to earn the next belt / sash).

X   Home Security and Defense

a.   Home Security

This is a chapter that the low-budget survivalist will love. Many of the things mentioned here consist of little, to no-cost.

Home security for the survivalist is basically the same as what you see in the contemporary society. All that the survivalism theme does is place more emphasis on it. For example, you may be in a safe neighborhood now, where you know all of your neighbors, and there is no crime to speak of. The idea behind preparedness is the fact that this situation can change, at least over time. Remember: Preparedness and survivalism are about being *proactive*, not simply *reactive*.

Years ago, one day, I was watching the Discovery Channel TV show *It Takes a Thief*, about two reformed former burglars who test people's yards and homes, by actually breaking into them, before installing their own security systems for the property owner. I was able to pick-up on some very basic concepts, and realized that my own home and back yard were extremely vulnerable.

One thing to remember is that any one single piece of security is not going to stop a burglar. A Brinks Security sign on your lawn by itself will not necessarily stop an intruder. Locked gates to your backyard may not stop a burglar. However, in combinations, and in layers of security, it will all create a composite that will at least make a criminal pick another location, if not extremely slow him down, to the point where he aborts the attempt, in mid-effort.

Being a foundational thinker, let's start from the ground-up, literally.

Take a look at your yard: Do you have any tools lying out in the open, or on the outside of your house, such as axes, shovels, saws, etc? Collect these all up, and place them in your garage, or a locked shed, immediately. These items can be used as weapons, or tools to break into your house. They can also have their own inherent value to some crack-head. Also, do you have really rocky/stony soil around your house? Same thing. Rocks, stones, and old pieces of cement landfill can be used as weapons against your house. Collect as many of these as you can, and secure them, hide them, or get rid of them, if possible. As a prepper, you should plan on re-utilizing these anyway, in the form of a graveled walkway, an outdoor fireplace project, etc. In the near term, a burglar could use these items. In a worst-case, societal collapse scenario: Your neighbors could be standing around your house, all pissed-off, because they think they have a right to your supplies (because you blew your OPSEC, somehow). All of a sudden, one of them finds some stones in your front yard, picks them up, and starts throwing them through your windows. All of a sudden, the rest of your neighbors join in...

From the TV show previously mentioned, I realized that we had our six-foot tall gate latches located on the outside of our fence gate, courtesy of the crew that originally built the fence. I removed these existing latches, and re-installed them on the other side. Granted, I had to reverse the side that secured to the gate, and to the post it secured to, but this was no problem. Second, I bought a four-pack of keyed-alike locks (meaning one key operates all four padlocks), and installed one on each gate, and the door to my shed. This makes it more convenient for other family members/retreat members to operate the locks from one key.

Another low/no-cost thing to do is to plant, or transplant thorny bushes under each window, and in likely avenues of approach, around your property. By avenue of approach, I mean routes where a bad guy is likely to approach your property, or house. There are many varieties of thorny plant, but my favorite is the good old Himalayan Blackberry, which needless to say, is very prolific here in the continental US. This is the most invasive plant I have ever come across, like something from another planet! As its vines grow, once their tips make contact with the ground, they immediately generate additional root systems. The vines create a natural form of concertina wire. I love them. They also form another use: Blackberries! From the season before writing this book, I picked enough ripe Blackberries to make and can 3 ½ quarts of Blackberry Jam (and some of the best you ever tasted). Yummy!

Himalayan Blackberry (Wikipedia)

When transplanting blackberries for instance, dig up as much of the root system as possible, as you would with any plant you are attempting to transplant. With blackberries, needless to say, due to their survivability, they will cut you some slack. Dig the holes where you want to put these guys, and throw a handful of chemical fertilizer, such as Miracle Grow, into the hole, with the plant. Also add a lot of water to the roots as you bury it. Initially, over a period of a couple of weeks at least, you will see these transplants die back. After this, however, you will see new growth coming from the roots of these transplants, just like a T1000 Terminator (from that movie) getting knocked down with a bunch of point blank .12 gauge rounds, then opening its eyes, and getting back up. Eventually, due to the addition of the chemical fertilizer, you will see stalks coming out of the ground that resemble some sort of one-inch diameter spiked medieval weapon.

In addition to an effective security barrier, blackberries are notable for their high nutritional contents of dietary fiber(the seeds), vitamin C, vitamin K, folic acid (a B vitamin), and the essential mineral manganese. They rank highly among fruits for antioxidant strength, particularly due to their dense contents of polyphenolic compounds, such as ellagic acid, tannins, ellagitannins, quercetin, gallic acid, anthocyanins and cyanidins. (Wikipedia).

Some people insist on more visually appealing thorny plants, such as Barberry. Barberry is more controllable, and easily trim-able. It is used commercially as a barrier plant around public buildings. Its thorns more closely resemble long sewing needles, rather than the painful and irritating effects of a Blackberry vine. However, barberry is not as effective a man-stopper as blackberry, as I can attest to having easily walked right through it, while doing photo shoots for this book (Ch. 16, Individual Tactical Techniques).

Barberry Thorns (Wikipedia)

When using plants, or any fencing, wire, etc. as obstacles, we need to remember how obstacles are used. The basic concept drilled into every US Army combat arms soldier is that obstacles have three distinct purposes:

- To block movement
- To delay movement
- To channelize (or "canalize," to use the military term) an intruder or opposing force into a more advantageous area, for the defender.

In some areas of your yard you may be able to successfully block a potential burglar with a transplanted patch of blackberry. For instance, if you are just now applying these concepts to your yard, you would want to prioritize by planting thorny bushes under your windows (blocking), then along the inside of any fence that borders a creek bed (delaying), or other concealable avenue of approach. In areas where you have no ability to directly observe an area, such as a side of your house where there are no windows, your priority should be to plant in this type of area that would block movement onto the property as much as possible, in order to canalize an intruder into a more open area, where they would be more exposed to your view, or other neighbors, passers-by, etc. Or, canalized at least to an area where you have electronic intrusion detection systems emplaced.

As for inside your home, make sure that at least any sliding glass doors have some sort of bar material, such as a wooden dowel, a piece of metal, etc. On many modern, energy efficient windows, there is already an effective lever that secures windows shut. However, if you live in an older house in particular (one with older, less energy-efficient aluminum window frames, for instance), then you should have a piece of wooden dowel or metal bar material in each window. For visual appeal and to confuse potential burglars, paint these wooden dowels in the same color as the window frame: Gloss white to match white plastic window frames, or metallic colored paint to match metal window frames.

If you are installing newer doors, or want to improve older ones, install wrap-around door security plates to your doors. Hopefully your exterior doors, including the one to your garage are already deadbolted. Security plates are basically just sleeves, made of sheet metal that are positioned around the door knob and the dead bolt on the door itself, and act as a composite layer around these bolt openings, making it harder for someone to kick or ram the door open. In addition, remove the little one-inch screws that attach the strike plates to the door frames, and replace them with ones that are at least three inches long. These longer screws will go into not just the door frame, but the frame of the house itself, again making it that much harder for someone to force the door open. Just make sure that you drill pilot holes for these longer screws, as you do not want to risk breaking these longer screws in half as you screw them into place.

In addition to these measures, you can install a sort of strike plate on steroids, on top of the existing strike plates on the door frame. These consist of a 1/8 inch thick piece of sheet metal, about two feet long and 1 ½ inches wide. Holes will need to be made in this material, to match the spacing of your dead bolt and door knob bolts. Only install something like this when you still have sufficient space between the door and the door frame.

In the photo above, a pistol, with corded hearing protection attached, along with a prepared statement for law enforcement is shown. The statement basically says that you will point out any witnesses and evidence, but will not speak to law enforcement outside the presence of an attorney. It is the opinion of this author that a firearm kept for this purpose should be unloaded, with loaded magazines or other ammunition kept out of the reach of children (to include grand-kids, etc).

Lastly, in the contemporary, slow-collapse environment, having a firearm ready for home defense is a matter of choice, based on children in the home, an imminent threat, etc. Based on the number of loved ones killed by accidental discharges (as compared to actual intruders), I do not recommend that everyone keep a firearm ready, for this purpose. Personally (and logically), I would rather be shot by an intruder, than living with the memory of having been responsible for the death of a loved one.

b.   Defendability

Now on to a more uniquely survivalist topic: Fortifying your property. If things go from bad to worse, in addition to the types of long-term collapse factors already mentioned, you will need to be prepared for everything from pairs of armed drug addict brigands, to highly skilled groups of former law enforcement and military personnel.

When planning a perimeter defense, think of it in terms of the "inside-out" In other words, place as much of your resources around an inner core, whether it is your house, or even just a room within your house. Use the example of the firebases that the US Army built during the Vietnam War: For instance, a core perimeter was formed around the command post (CP), where a concentrated amount of firepower and obstacles were placed. Other perimeter rings were then placed around this one: Wire obstacles, fighting positions, etc. So in other words, they always built at least one perimeter inside-of-a-perimeter, as a final fallback position. Home defendability should be thought of the same way, prioritizing the home itself, then working out from there.

We basically want to get our hands on as much military information on this subject as possible, in the form of military FM's (field manuals), etc. The following diagrams should provide some food for thought.

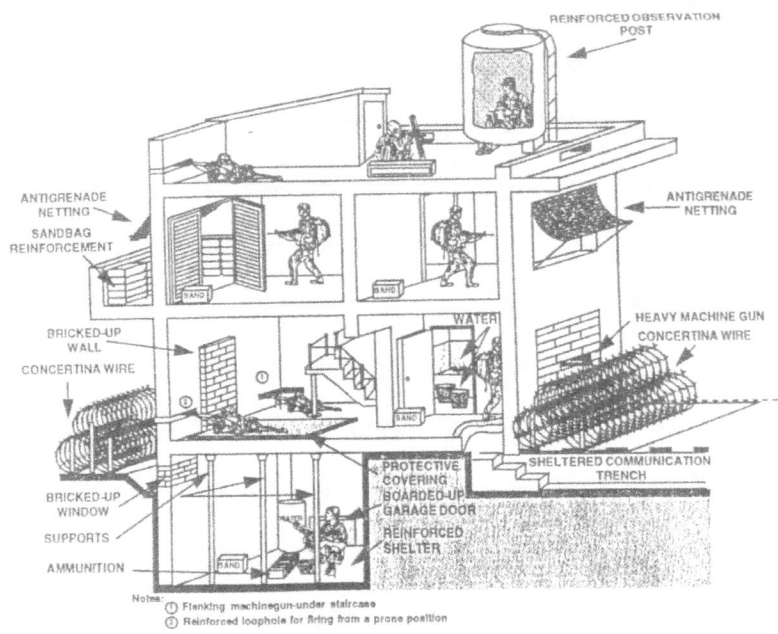

REINFORCED OBSERVATION POST

ANTIGRENADE NETTING

SANDBAG REINFORCEMENT

ANTIGRENADE NETTING

BRICKED-UP WALL

CONCERTINA WIRE

WATER

HEAVY MACHINE GUN

CONCERTINA WIRE

PROTECTIVE COVERING

BOARDED-UP GARAGE DOOR

REINFORCED SHELTER

SHELTERED COMMUNICATION TRENCH

BRICKED-UP WINDOW

SUPPORTS

AMMUNITION

Notes: ① Flanking machinegun-under staircase
② Reinforced loophole for firing from a prone position

Figure 16-4. Example defense of building.

Fortifying a building (From US Army Field Manual 90-10: *An Infantryman's Guide to Combat in Built-up Areas*)

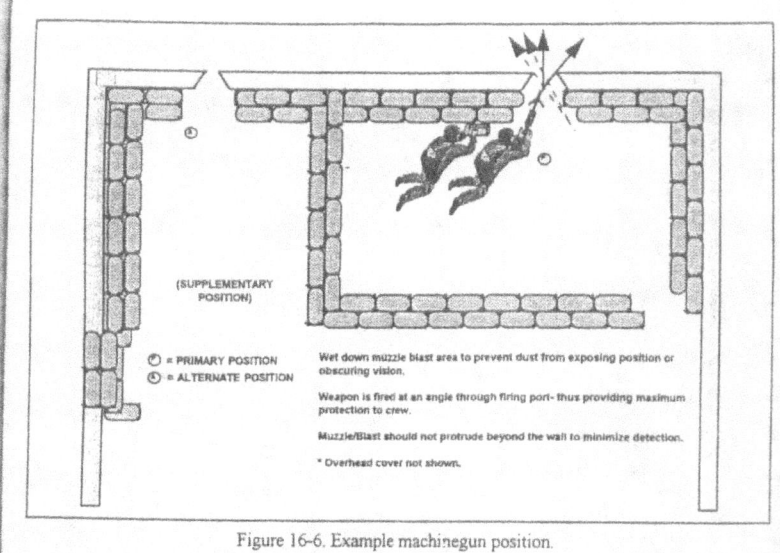

(SUPPLEMENTARY POSITION)

○ = PRIMARY POSITION
○ = ALTERNATE POSITION

Wet down muzzle blast area to prevent dust from exposing position or obscuring vision.

Weapon is fired at an angle through firing port- thus providing maximum protection to crew.

Muzzle/Blast should not protrude beyond the wall to minimize detection.

* Overhead cover not shown.

Figure 16-6. Example machinegun position.

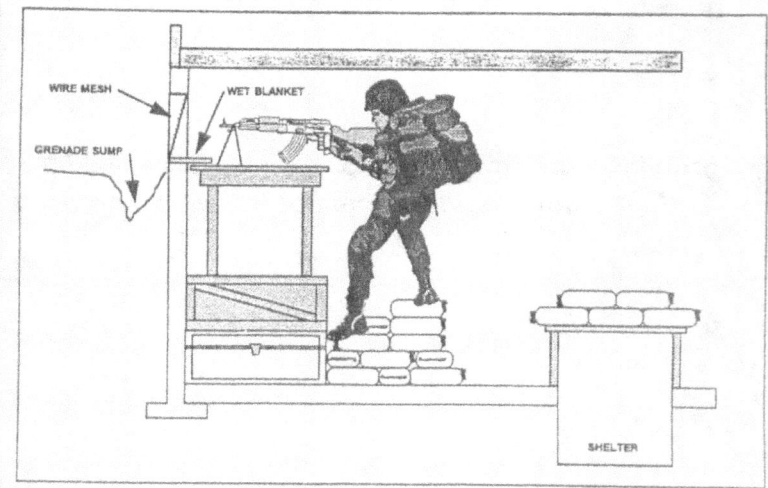

WIRE MESH

WET BLANKET

GRENADE SUMP

SHELTER

Figure 16-7. Example cellar firing position

16-21

Examples of first floor and cellar (basement) firing positions (US Army Field Manual 90-10)

Some people may think that some of the military techniques

shown are not applicable to defending your "bugged-in" home, or retreat: Think again! For instance, we want to use everything shown regarding protections from hand grenades. Someone may aim for the basement air vent that you are firing through, with a Molotov Cocktail. Or, God forbid, the real thing, stolen from the military, to include CS gas, flash-bangs, etc. Also notice the use of concertina wire: In our case, it would also keep someone from sneaking up on our basement opening, in order to open-up at close range with a pistol, etc.

We have already touched on the use of thorny plants as barriers. Another favorite of mine is the use of wire obstacles. After reading Jim Rawles' *Patriots: A Novel of Survival in the Coming Collapse*, I realized that barbed wire, razor wire, military-issue concertina wire, etc. was going to be "worth its weight in gold," literally, after a societal collapse, such as the one described in *Patriots*. However, for the suburban survivalist, one would not want to deploy this stuff in the contemporary environment. While it would not only draw unneeded attention from the neighbors, there are city and county ordinances that forbid the use of razor wire on the tops of fences, etc. Therefore, the ideal plan is to have a place to safely store these items, where they are in some out-of-the-way place, where they won't make contact with other items.

If you are in a situation, like present-day Detroit, Michigan for instance, you could position barbed-wire or rolls of razor wire on the *inside* of your fence, just below the top of it. This would keep it from being seen from outside your yard, until someone tries to hop over your fence, and then sees the wire. When that person sees that they are about to jump down into this stuff, they may just change their mind. If they do jump over a fence into this stuff, just as well, except now they may be in more of a panic, trying to get back over the fence, and out of that yard. In an absence of the rule of law scenario, this would be the perfect time to engage targets with weapons fire.

One of the beautiful things about storing spools of barbed

wire or rolls of concertina is that in the event of societal collapse, you will likely become a hero, if your community, or neighborhood actually pulls together (as I have mentioned in other areas of this book, something that I'm not willing to put a lot of money on, in our current society). Hopefully, you're not already known as the neighbor who "is preparing for the end of the world." In either case, if your neighbors are scared shitless, but beginning to organize, and they see you appearing with this stuff, you *will* become a hero.

In the late 2000's CBS TV series *Jericho* for instance, the character of Hawkins (my favorite) kept a pretty low profile after having moved into the town, with his estranged family. After he began forming relationships and helping out, the nearby town of New Burn put Jericho under attack, starting a localized resource war. As the town of Jericho tried preparing for this attack with very few resources, Hawkins then appeared with entire military arms room racks full of M16's, and ammunition. He instantly became a hero to the entire community! Yes, this was just a fictional TV series, but fiction has a strange way of becoming fact in our culture (and yes, like every other survivalist in the US in 2006-08, I was watching every episode on the edge of my seat. Normally, I do not even watch TV).

However, this can be a double-edged sword, as well. If you appear to be the only male adult actually prepared for this type of event after having tipped your hand as a survivalist, then the other neighbors may correctly assume that you have other stored goods, and resources. It will greatly depend on the situation, and what you actually have for a neighborhood. If the situation is nationwide or global, and the situation continues to deteriorate, then you will also have to factor-in decisions: Do you then "bug out" (more on this later in the book) with all of your supplies, or hole-up against what is left of your neighbors, who may notice that you are still living in relative comfort?

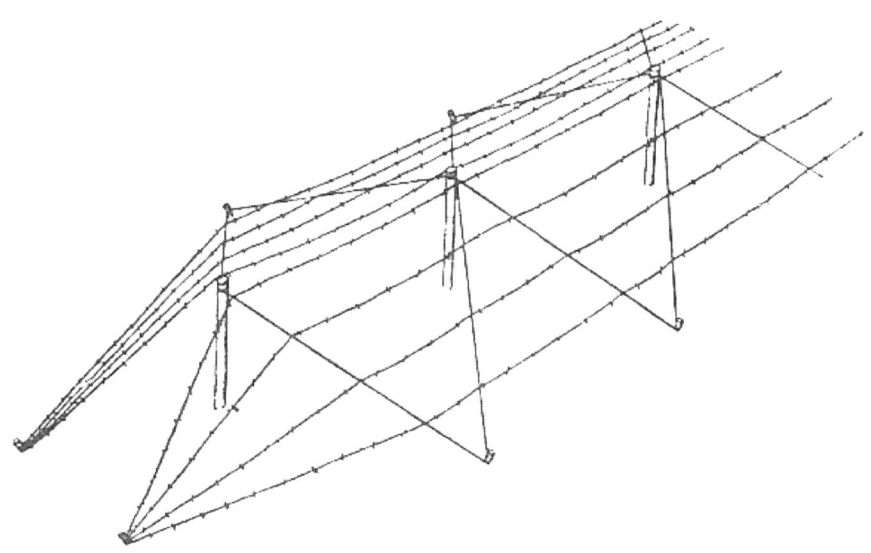

Double-apron barbed-wire arrangement (US Army)

Hopefully this chapter has provided a basic guide, as well as some food for thought, if / when we have a societal disaster. As previously mentioned, based on historical precedents, we may not get a fast crash. After all, we are already in a second Great Depression, based on the pre-adjusted figures for unemployment, GDP, CPI, etc. However, as some anthropological evidence has uncovered, societies in decline have had fast crash moments, such as the sacking of Rome by the Visigoths in the 5th Century AD, the final moments of the Mayan Civilization, the Anasazi, and other chaotic moments at the very end of a civilization.

XI   Mental Attitude

"I don't give a fuck about your war...Or your President"

- Kurt Russell as Snake Plisskin from the movie *Escape from New York* (1981)

The thought for this chapter came one morning while I was talking to my mechanic, working on one of my vehicles. The guy was just jabbering away non-stop, with non-relevant information about other people's vehicles, etc. Although he and his partner in their shop had already done excellent work on my vehicle, I had already read the tell-tale signs of methamphetamine use on the part of this mechanic. I knew I was going to lose it at one point, so sure enough; I went "Samuel L. Jackson" (i.e., *Pulp Fiction*) on him:

"Look! Shut the fuck up and listen to me, alright!
You need to lay off the fucking meth! I know I'm
sounding harsh this morning, but I've see it before,
alright?"

At least the guy did not deny my accusation. I then explained to him my original idea from the previous day, for injecting fuel from a fuel can directly into the fuel line, in order to get the engine warmed-up, in order to run the crappy blend of poorly centrifuged vegetable oil and diesel out of my fuel tank, that I had acquired from a complete idiot (who claimed he had a Masters in Engineering degree). When I visited the mechanic moments later with a fuel container, everything was good, and I did acknowledge again that he had already done good work on the air-conditioning system that I had them restore (I never apologized for calling him a meth-head, however).

I'm not saying that we should all treat everyone we meet like this. Unless we are already a survivalist hermit living in a hidden underground location, then we are going to be interacting with people. In other words, as things continue to decline, we are going to see more theft, more drug addiction, more people trying to pull scams, more people trying to do hard sells, and more desperate people in general. All the things that already make Umerican society so wonderful. Therefore, we need to be more mentally aggressive. As mentioned elsewhere in this book, I try to fix things that I see wrong in my environment.

Personally, I have had a lot to be angry about, during my lifetime. Abandonment (not just by an immediate parent, but by extended relatives on both sides, as well), then abuse at the hands of strangers (foster parents), then being a young parent with no extended family for help. I decided that as an adult and as a survivalist, that I should use that basic emotional component not only in interactions with people, but as a healthy, emotional component in assertiveness, leadership, etc.

One thing that I have learned in life is that if you don't have your mental guard up, and are mentally alert, that people will take advantage of you. It's literally like an aura, that people can actually see, either way. It is a sad commentary that says that we have to conduct ourselves in this manner, but this is what human beings have been reduced to in our industrialized society: Constantly looking for weakness amongst our fellow human beings. I don't believe for a second that human beings were meant to relate like this to each other. It is definitely not apparent in tribal societies that still exist.

In addition to not trusting anyone, another important mental trait, more encompassing, and just as important, is just basically not giving a rat's ass. About anything. I'm not talking here about yourself, your family, or your home, or your community. I mean the nightly network news, politics, the latest style or fashion, the latest hand-held electronic gadget, or the latest person going postal in the middle of a movie theater (there will be many more of them in the future as our current state of societal decline accelerates, to the point where they no longer make news).

Also, if you're pissed about the government (federal, local, etc), the system, society as a whole, etc, then the best form of retaliation is to ignore them, period. Just get out of their way, as they become bankrupt, and irrelevant. In other words, as the famous Russian writer and activist Alexander Solzhenitsyn once said "Don't believe them, don't fear them, don't ask anything of them."

One of my favorite movies of all time is John Carpenter's *Escape from New York* (1981). In an interview accompanying the 2003 Special Edition DVD, John Carpenter described the character of Snake Plisskin, and how he fit into the dystopic environment that Carpenter created (italicized words are the from the speaker's own emphasis):

> "I think I probably made everybody corrupt in this world. *Every single person corrupt* in this world, entirely a nihilistic corruption blanket of this future. And Snake Plisskin is really the only man with honor, because he doesn't care about anybody."

Wow, that doesn't sound like our current socio-political-economic world, does it? Kurt Russell (who played Snake Plisskin) also mentioned when interviewed:

> "Ultimately he's my favorite character, because I think he's the most complex. He's a fantasy character. He does things that are *fantasy*. They're not the things that you and I are going to do in our life, or *shouldn't* do in our life. When we want to kill somebody, we shouldn't do that. The world would be a very bad place to live in. But he lives in a fantasy world. He lives in a world where if you *don't* have that attitude, you're going to go. So he

has no question about what he has to do."

As history has taught us, science fiction/fantasy has a strange way of becoming science fact. This vision of John Carpenter's has since played out in places like Russia during the collapse of the Soviet Union, the Bosnian Civil War, the Iraq and Afghan occupations (both Soviet *and* US), Hurricanes Katrina and Sandy, etc. Although a little outdated (the future in this movie takes place in the year 1997), I still think that John Carpenter nailed it in this great allegory of our present society (a state of constant foreign war even exists in this film!), the screenplay of which was originally written in the aftermath of Watergate and The Vietnam War.

Unfortunately, a majority of Umericans are weak-minded. This is evidenced by what they now wear. I can't stand how every guy out there feels compelled to fit in, so they have to wear the "baby clothes"[3] and the tattoos (oh, and the idiot Umerican crowd also has to wear the shorts, in order to show-off the tattoos on their legs, regardless of what the rest of their body looks like). All this, in addition to the phony little Shakespeare beards, the earrings in weird places, and of course, the dumb-looking hat with the sunglasses on top.

Women (of all ages) are guilty of the same thing, with the tattoos, earrings in their faces (which I consider outright hideous), and flip-flops with painted toenails (no matter how ugly their feet are, to begin with. Most should simply wear shoes).

Whenever I see this need to visually fit-in, I think of Abraham Maslow's theory of Self-Concept. In other words, there seems to be no sense of their "outside self," or awareness of how others actually perceive them. This weak mindedness is the reason why many of us are survivalists in the first place: These people can be dangerous if formed into one mindless mass of people. We have

---

3   Borrowed from James Howard Kunstler, referring to oversized t-shirts and shorts, going

past the knees. Also known as "pajama pants."

already seen this in the unprepared masses in the aftermath of Hurricane Sandy in October of 2012, the fear-infused run on firearms and ammunition in 2012-2013, etc. Or, for that matter, the people who were stirred-up by demagogues in the former Yugoslavia in the early 1990's, creating the bloodiest conflict (The Bosnian War) in Europe since WWII.

If you are reading this book, then you are probably already aware of a Matrix-like reality, courtesy of the politicians, bankers and CEO's who all want to maintain the status quo for their own benefit (to include a dumbed-down American public) , and are well aware that we are living within a decaying socio-economic system and culture. If you are angry about what you see going on around you, and within our un-representative government (i.e., the bailouts, the wars, etc.,) then use this anger constructively to care for yourself, your loved ones, and your community, if possible.

XII Survival Kits

a. Small Survival Kits

We need survival kits that have what we realistically need in them, whether we're stuck downtown during some unforeseen event, or while traveling by car, motorcycle, bicycle, or public transportation, during a crisis. More than likely, we'll be in an urbanized/suburbanized environment.

The following are two survival kits I've put together: A compact, cargo or jacket pocket-sized survival kit, and a larger, emergency food supply kit.

For the pocket-sized kit, I basically dumped the original contents of this gasketed, waterproof container, which included fishing line and hooks, a tiny cheapo excuse of a multi-tool (I usually have a Gerber multi-tool on my belt, anyway), a candle, and a cheap incandescent flashlight. A good, small survival kit should have the things that you would actually use during both emergencies and non-emergencies. It should be waterproof, and able to float.

The pocket-sized kit pictured on p. 102 consists of the following (with explanations):

• *Corded* Ear Plugs: You never know when you may need them, for traveling in a noisy vehicle, around noisy machinery, firing a weapon, explosions, etc. Personally, I'd rather lose my life than my hearing, but that's just me. In particular, people who travel armed, or may need to lend their motorcycle helmet to a passenger, etc., should consider carrying hearing protection. When needed, these are to be worn at-the-ready, around the neck. I had a pair of these around my neck at all times while in Libya, being around constant, unannounced test fires of anti-aircraft guns, etc. You can also string earplugs together using the inner strand material from 550 parachute cord. Remember, each individual strand has 35 pounds of tensile strength.

• Water purification tablets: Nothing is more important than staying hydrated, except breathing. A single bottle of water purification tablets should be more than enough for yourself and others, in a short-term scenario. If you find yourself in a longer scenario, well, it sucks to be them.

• Ibuprofen / aspirin: How many times have we been at work, and suddenly had a headache? Also useful for temporary pain relief from injuries.

• A single / mini LED (i.e., keychain LED, minus the keychain) flashlight. Although many of us already carry one on our keychain, the one in our kit will ensure having one that will light up an entire room, if necessary. Also for non-emergencies. Speaking from experience: Have you ever had a power outage at your workplace, when people needed to use the restroom?

• Matches: for lighting candles, starting fires, etc. Also, regular book matches can be split down the middle, actually doubling the number of matches in a book, in an extreme situation (sometimes you actually can learn something watching The Discovery Channel).

• Compact toothbrush, toothpaste, and dental floss: During an emergency, I feel that the most important form of hygiene is dental hygiene.

• Band-aids: Small ones for small cuts, larger ones for gashes.

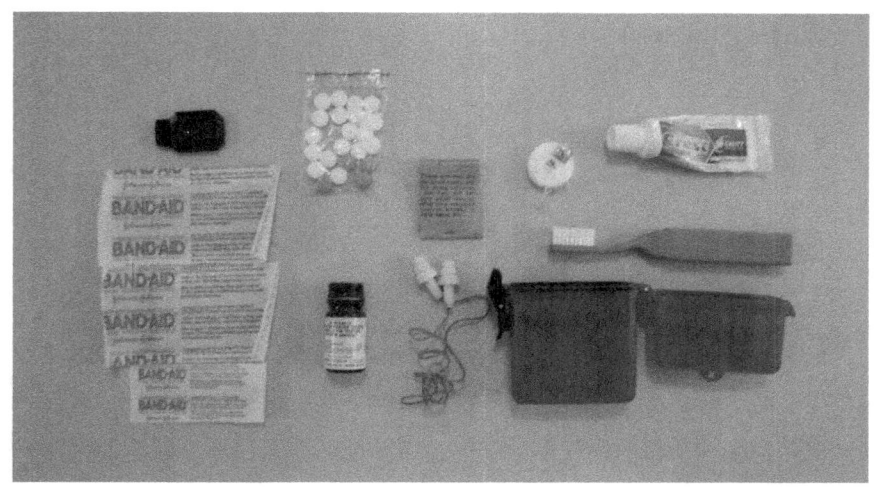

Pocket-size survival kit, with waterproof / floatable container

Another thing to consider with this type of kit: Unless you're in a totally dirt-poor environment, there are always resources around you. Your own small survival kit should simply provide a small backup core of essential supplies. Only use these supplies when necessary.

An emergency food kit should be lightweight, without excess material. This is why I generally do not like military MRE's (as previously mentioned) as a survival / preparedness form of nourishment. Don't get me wrong; they're ideal for what they were designed for: Conveniently packaged, highly fortified sealed meals, designed to be consumed under training and combat conditions.

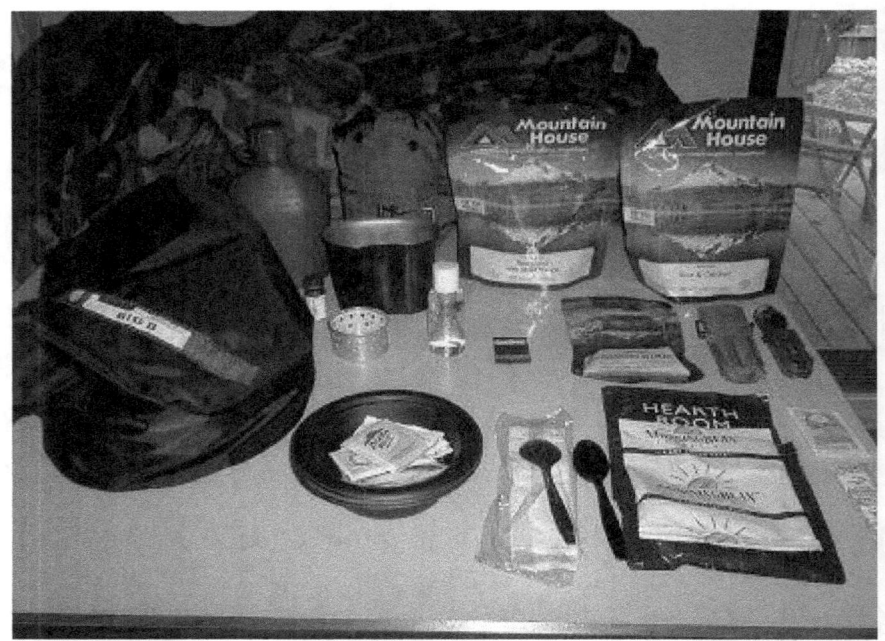

Emergency Food kit, consisting of canteen, canteen cup and pouch, along with two Mountain House Main Courses and a dessert, an OD green folding knife-type mess kit, hotel coffee packs, and a "cat" stove with alcohol, along with other condiments, and a carry bag.

My emergency food kit consists of the following:

• Mountain House or similar dehydrated meals. They're lightweight. The only water we should be hauling is for drinking, if at all possible (If you're on a lower budget, canned food is OK). Although there is also a "use by" date on these as well, dehydrated food generally has a virtually unlimited shelf life. Also, try not to use a whole meal at a time, if you are by yourself. These meal packs are usually meant for two people, and are packaged in resealable pouches.

• Canteen, canteen cup and canteen pouch: Or whatever you want to haul your water in, along with something you can heat it in, and carry it all in. My canteen pouch is a typical, older ALICE-type, designed to attach to pistol belts, backpacks, etc. The carrier also has a dedicated outside pocket for a bottle of water purification tablets.

• Alcohol "cat" stove, with a shatterproof container of denatured alcohol for fuel: For boiling water for the Mountain House meals, hot drinks, re-heating food, etc. I discovered in Misrata, Libya that automotive gasoline treatment also works well as a fuel for these simple stoves. Be very careful using these types of fuel additives, however, since they tend to be pure methanol, which burns without visible flame.

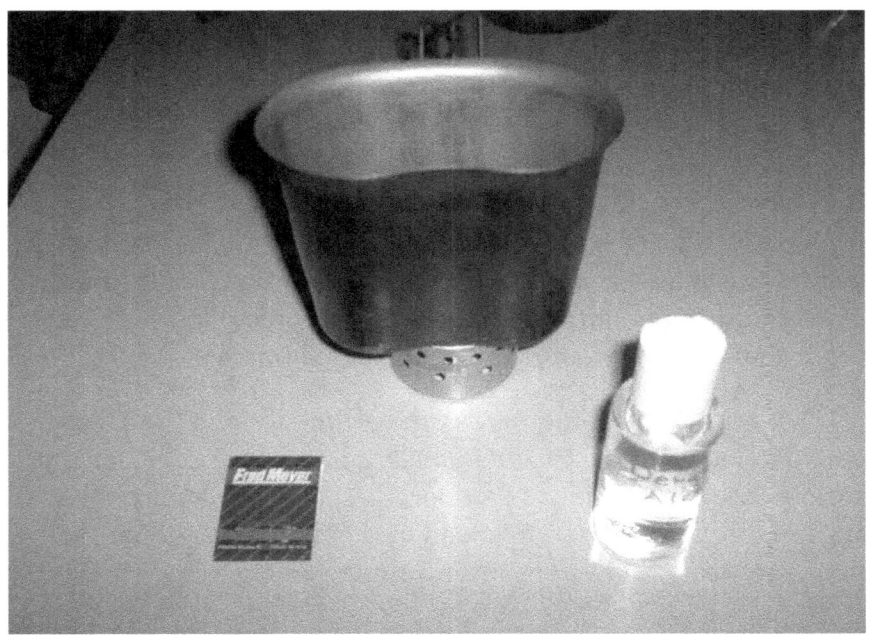

"Cat" stove with matches, container of denatured alcohol, and canteen cup (note that the stove works by having the pan, or canteen cup in this case, sitting directly on top of the stove).

• Instant Coffee. Nowadays, instant coffee tends to be just as good as the real thing. It should after all, since it is just real coffee that has been freeze-dried: One of the first commonly-used forms of freeze-dried food, originally made for the military during World War Two. I used to use some of the saved coffee packs from hotels, but these take up space, and the ground coffee inside of them tends to get old, over time.

• Matches, water purification tablets, a knife-type mess kit, quality paper-ware plates, saved condiments from fast food, etc.

These survival kit examples should provide food-for-thought for your own realistically planned survival kits. When getting information from any source, think about what works best for *your* situation / potential situation.

b. Get Home Bags

A "get home" bag is essentially an emergency kit that you keep in the vehicle that you drive to work each day, or at your place of work. The purpose of this kit is in expectation of any event that interferes with your ability to get home.

For instance, what if there is an earthquake and the bridges between your workplace and home are taken out? Or, what if, as socio-economic conditions deteriorate, that we suddenly have a collapse of the US Dollar, followed by an instant shutdown of all public services, followed by instant rioting and looting?

A get home bag should consist of the following (in order of importance):

- At least one quart of bottled water.
- Water purification tablets, or a personal water filtration system, in the event of an extended emergency, and the need to scavenge for water.

- A standard, military-issue one-quart canteen, as a practical drinking vessel. While on the front line west of Misrata during the 2011 Libyan Revolutionary War, every other journalist had these cutesy-looking metal water bottles. They all developed leaks. I was the only one out there staying hydrated. You can't re-invent a good canteen.
- Some high-protein, calorie-dense food in the form of energy bars, peanut butter and crackers, etc.
- A handgun, with at least two loaded magazines, and an additional 50-round box of ammunition.
- A backpack to contain all of this stuff in. Not a suitcase, or shoulder bag, etc. As preppers / survivalists, we want everything "manpackable," meaning, "on our backs." Granted, some people are not physically capable of walking with a backpack, so small, wheeled pieces of luggage would suffice, in this case. One of the main reasons to get in shape as a survivalist.
- A small first-aid kit.

This should serve as a basic packing list for a get home bag, since space is a consideration in most people's vehicles. You may want to add other items, such as a sleeping bag, blankets, hygiene items, etc. In addition, you may want to add a carbine conversion attachment for your handgun, or an additional weapon, like a Henry Arms .22 LR AR-7 Survival Rifle (more on this in the chapter on firearms). Again, think in terms of your specific situation.

c.   **"Bugout" Bags**

Although I am not a fan of the bugging out concept (more on

this later), there are times for it, in the event of a natural disaster, chemical spill, etc. This should consist of a large backpack, preferably a large military issue bag, like the older generation US military issue ALICE (large size) pack, or even a simple military issue duffel bag (these essentially create their own frame, as you stuff them). Although a duffel bag is not a tactical bag, you can stuff a lot into it. Or, as little as you want into it as well, since they can virtually double as a day pack.

This bag will be big, needless to say. We're talking, as a minimum:

- Canteens: One-quart, if not two quart "Jungle" Canteens.
- Water treatment: Tablets, personal filtration systems, etc.
- Sleeping bag with a sleeping pad, either a foam polypad or self-inflating (expanding foam-filled) mattress.
- Food, in the form of dehydrated meals. Here, a couple of MRE's added would not be a bad idea (mainly for some of the self-contained items that you may have forgotten elsewhere in the bag). Also foods like high-energy bars, etc.
- A Main Battle Rifle (MBR), with the upper and lower receivers (such as with an AR rifle) taken apart to include at least six loaded magazines, all inside of the backpack. This is also based on whatever you can afford for a long-barreled weapon, whether it is a .12 ga. shotgun, an AR rifle, a surplus bolt-action, etc. This is also based on what you can fit in your trunk, conceal inside the bag, etc. This is why I like pistol-caliber carbines (short rifles) for the urban survivalist, in particular.

This is all in addition of course, to the items previously mentioned in other kits. I think you get the idea here: You are going to have to be in good shape, as all of this stuff has to be man-packable. Of course, you could put this stuff on a wheeled luggage cart, or in a piece of wheeled luggage. However, this will limit your mobility, and make you visually stick-out more, making you vulnerable to observation, attacks, etc.

What to Have in Your Vehicle

Again, being a foundational thinker, let's start with the basics, because many Americans do not. How many people call themselves preppers, yet do not even have a spare tire in their car? Or a tire iron? The numbers can be surprising.

Every car should have in it:

- A full-size spare tire. If you have a "space saver" wheel/tire combo in your car, then go to a junkyard, get a used wheel, and take that to a tire shop and get a tire mounted and balanced on it. Then throw away the space saver wheel. They're a waste of time. Now you don't even have to worry about tire rotations. It will happen whenever you get a flat or worn tire. For collapse scenarios, I highly recommend *two* spare tires for each vehicle

- Tire iron, jack, and a safety jack. They don't have to be the original, perfect set that came with the vehicle. On one of my trucks, my tire iron consists of a socket wrench (not an actual ratchet; a ratchet might internally break) with the proper socket fitting for my lug nuts. Also, for women, the physically impaired, etc., I recommend the use of a breaker bar, with the correct socket fitting for your lug nuts. This is simply a longer handle, to attach a socket fitting to, for leverage.

- A flashlight. On some trucks, for instance, you simply can't access the spare tire in the dark, without one. My favorites are the single keychain LED lights. The ones I use actually run on six volts, and have the brightest light, for the smallest physical footprint. Keep one of these in your glove box (hopefully, you already have something like this on your keychain, at least). One really neat product are the rechargeable LED flashlights that plug directly into your cigarette lighter. For collapse scenarios, my favorite shade of LED lighting is green. Red has always been the traditional shade of subdued military lighting, but green, being an earth-tone, is better for two reasons: It is harder for the untrained eye to notice at a distance, and it is night vision device compatible.

- A complete set of spare keys for the ignition, tailgate locks, locking canopies, etc. These should be on their own key ring, inside of a hidden magnetic box, somewhere underneath the frame of the vehicle. Be creative!

- A one-gallon jug of drinkable water. Not distilled water. There are no trace minerals in distilled water, just re-condensed H2O.

- A sleeping bag, with a good temperature rating (i.e., zero degrees F.).

Again, everyone has different living situations. This chapter should serve as a basic guide for what you should have on you, in a purpose-specific pack, and in your vehicle.

XIII. Firearms

a. Which Ones are the Best for Your Situation?

Firearms are just like vehicles: Certain ones are better for certain applications than others. Some are more appropriate for an individual than others. Personally owned firearms say a lot about a person, much as a car does.

Different firearms are also required for different environments. The .12 gauge shotgun is ideal for home defense, but not for long-range engagements. At the other end, a long-range sniper rifle is not appropriate for most Survivalists, as many within the culture would like to think. What are you going to do on the other side of societal collapse? Shoot at every human being you happen to notice at 800 yards? Not to belittle long-range shooting skills. We should all be working on those, as they may be needed during a long-term societal emergency.

There is a reason why I de-prioritized this subject; in the order that these chapters are presented. Many people without formal experience with weapons have this innate fascination with firearms, to the point where their priorities are totally out of whack.

For instance, based on my consulting experience, what is the point of having more than a handgun for personal self defense, if you have poor eyesight, due to the need for new glasses or surgery? What if you have bought a Kevlar helmet, body armor, and an assault rifle, but are not physically fit enough to move 50-feet outside of your house with this stuff on? Not to mention a personal combat load of six-to-eight loaded 30-round magazines, in addition to one locked-into the weapon, full water canteens, etc.

We'll begin here with firearm cartridges, rather than referring directly to the weapons that use them. This allows for a more fundamental understanding for the novices out there, as the US firearm market is like a used car market on steroids: Everyone is fascinated by them and wants them, yet hardly anyone actually understands their technical aspects, or proper application (one of the many reasons for the proliferation of firearms in the US). Also, I will be using proper terminology, and not using the word "gun" in this writing. What can I say? I'm a product of the US Army myself, and the US Army never uses the term "gun," other than referring to machine guns, and other crew-served weapons.

Jim Rawles, of SurvivalBlog.com fame, and the author of *Patriots: A Novel of Survival in the Coming Collapse*, insists that everyone who can afford one arm themselves with an assault rifle, preferably in Winchester .308 caliber (7.62 NATO). I understand his logic here, as good old 7.62 NATO is more of an old school, man-killer of a cartridge.

Another caliber is the more ubiquitous Remington .223 (5.56 NATO) round. This rifle cartridge is the most popular throughout the US, based on the proliferation of AR15's (the civilian version of the M16) that have been sold in recent years. The rifles and ammunition are lightweight, with light recoil, making them easy to operate among women, children, etc. This is in addition to the relative low cost of the ammunition.

However, one needs to understand why the 5.56 NATO cartridge and the M16 were developed. In the 1950's, the US Army was well aware of the fact that if you wounded an enemy on the battlefield rather than outright killing them, that it tied-up as many as eight other enemy personnel. There were also other reasons:

- The Army wanted a smaller, hypervelocity .22 caliber cartridge, to decrease an infantryman's overall equipment weight, while increasing overall firepower.

- It was concluded during World War II (primarily between the Soviets and the Germans) that the overwhelming majority of combat occurred within 300 yards.

This means one thing, folks: That the 5.56 NATO cartridge is intended as a *wounding round*, more than an outright man-stopper. Don't get me wrong; at roughly 2300 feet per second, this round will kill (particularly in the absence of medical attention), just like any other high velocity rifle cartridge. Particularly based on shot placement. But we must consider this basic fact.

Another popular cartridge is the 7.62x39mm (in this reference, "7.62" refers to the bullet diameter, while "x39mm" refers to the physical length of the overall cartridge, meaning that this cartridge is shorter in length than 7.62 NATO, which is 7.62x51mm). This is the cartridge of the world famous Soviet designed AK-47, and its variants. As I alluded to earlier, the Soviets were well aware of the typical distances that infantry combat was waged in. We have to understand that the Russians earned a PhD in land warfare, having fought the overwhelming bulk of the German Army non-stop from 1941-1945, in the most massive, and intense land warfare in human history. During the Cold War, the Soviets developed infantry weapons and weapons systems that have dictated how wars have been fought ever since.

AK-47, with cartridges and magazines (Source: Wikipedia)

The AK-47 (and its variants) is the most popular assault rifle in the world. I love Nicholas Cages' reference to the rifle in the movie *Lord of War*:

> Of all the weapons in the vast Soviet arsenal, nothing was more profitable than *Avtomat Kalashnikova*, model of year 1947, more commonly known as the AK-47, or Kalashnikov. It's the world's most popular assault rifle. A weapon all fighters love. An elegantly simple nine-pound amalgamation of forged steel and plywood. It doesn't break, jam, or overheat. It will shoot whether it's covered in mud, or filled with sand. It's so easy, even a child can use it. And they do.
>
> The Soviets put the gun on a coin. Mozambique put it on their flag. Since the end of The Cold War, the Kalashnikov has become the Russian people's greatest export. After that comes vodka, caviar, and suicidal novelists. One thing's for sure: Nobody was lining up to buy their cars.

To be more precise, sometime after the end of The Cold War, the Soviets stopped exporting AK's, as they were becoming less profitable (compared to other weapons systems), due to the global arms market having already been saturated with AK's, other third-world countries manufacturing them, etc. Also, the AK has traditionally been made from stamped parts (with the exception of high-quality Bulgarian-manufactured AK's, whose receivers are milled from solid steel), and solid pinewood.

Although Mikhail Kalashnikov, a young Tank Commander in the Soviet Army is credited with designing the AK-47 while recovering from combat injuries, the weapon has an uncanny resemblance to the German Sturmgewhr (StG) 44. The StG 44 design was specifically based on requests from German infantryman on the Eastern Front, for a more practical, modern combat rifle. The Sturmgewhr (pronounced "sturmgevher") was the very first of the modern, selective-fire, gas operated assault rifles.

Sturmgewhr (StG) 44 (source: Wikipedia)

The other performance aspect of the AK is the cartridge it shoots: The 7.62x39mm cartridge was actually designed prior to the development of the AK. Although not necessarily known for its accuracy, the wound effects of the 7.62x39mm cartridge are devastating. Even in the present day, American Iraq and Afghan War veterans can attest to having whole limbs severed by this round.

Years ago, as an older teenager serving active-duty in the US Army, I thought that the civilian versions of these assault rifles were ridiculous, since they were primarily designed for military, fully-automatic (meaning one pull of the trigger unleashes a controllable stream of bullets) use. The civilian versions of these weapons are limited to semi-automatic fire (one round fired with one pull of the trigger). However, as survivalists, we really do not want to concern ourselves with fully-automatic fire. In the hands of a minimally trained individual, it can cause an extreme waste of ammunition. The original military versions of these rifles were intended for controlled, three-round bursts, in order to create a shotgun-like effect on a target. When going through Army Infantry Basic Training at age 17, we were required to do an additional rifle qualification, with the M16 on full auto, using three-round bursts, with an aluminum bipod attached. As I can attest, this is a very

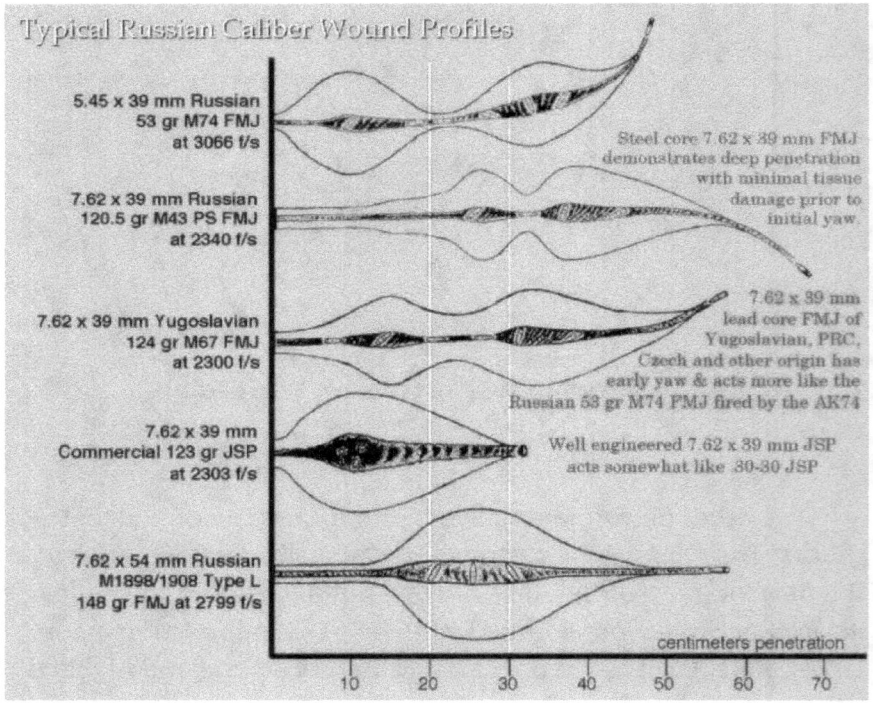

Wound profiles of the following calibers: 5.45x39mm (AK-74, top), 7.62x39mm (AK-47, AKM, middle three), and 7.62x54mm (Mosin-Nagant, SVD Dragunov, bottom). Source: COL Martin Fackler, US Army (Wikipedia)

effective and quick way of hitting a distant target with a rifle. As survivalists (again, as compared to soldiers), we do not have unlimited lines of supply, and have to operate accordingly. Not that there is any harm in having a fully-automatic weapon in your inventory, if you happen to come across one, pre-or-post collapse.[4]

b. My Favorite Assault Rifle Cartridge: 5.45mm Russian

Being a fan of the incredibly inexpensive Russian 5.45 x 39 mm military round, I thought I would mention it here, along with a recommendation for a good quality AR15 upper for this round.

Weapons makers in the US have never wanted to admit it, but in the early 1970's, the Soviet Union developed a highly engineered, yet incredibly inexpensive round, based on our 5.56mm NATO, yet much more ballistically improved, as well as destructive. Many people are still not aware that the Russian 5.45x39mm Soviet round has been the Russian/Soviet Army's main battle rifle cartridge since the mid-1970's.

Cheap to manufacture with a steel cartridge case, these rounds were designed for penetration and tumbling, due to a hollow cavity inside the tip of the bullet, in front of a comparatively large steel core, similar to 5.56 NATO M885 AP (Armor Piercing).

This round is also compatible with 5.56mm AR15 magazines: Other AR15 uppers in different calibers normally require different, dedicated magazines. You may want to stick with 27-28 rounds of 5.45mm in a 5.56mm magazine, since the case on the 5.45 round is .020" larger than 5.56 NATO.

---

[4]   Fully-automatic firearms, suppressors, certain threaded attachments, and short (sawed-off) shotguns currently require a federal tax stamp and registration with the Bureau of Alcohol, Tobacco, Firearms & Explosives.

My 5.45mm weapon system of choice is the M&P15R - Smith & Wesson's 5.45x39mm Upper Assembly for the AR-15. This is a high-quality, American-made AR upper, specially designed to fire the old Soviet surplus ammunition.

Going out to a rock quarry with an excess of 200 yards of range, I had set-up some water-filled two-liter pop bottles right at 200 and 212 yards. After checking my zero at 100 yards, I was hitting these with little effort (more like watching them explode, through my tubular red dot sight). And, aiming *directly at* them. There was no noticeable bullet drop, even at 200 yards.

Preppers and survivalists should consider the 5.45 mm Soviet cartridge, whether with the reviewed AR15 upper, or with a quality AK-74 (like the Polish Tantal line of AK-74's). The factory vacuum-sealed and stackable Soviet spam cans and two-can crates are uniquely suited for the survivalist's ammunition stockpile (you can tell the Soviets were serious about surviving WWIII). Jim Rawles at SurvivalBlog.com even refers to this cartridge as "The round of the future."[5]

c. Pistol Carbines for urban / suburban dwellers

Another area that I would like to cover is pistol carbines. These are basically short rifles that fire a pistol cartridge. Ballisticly, these will give you roughly 20 % more accuracy and range, for the same given cartridge, as compared to a pistol. These weapons are effective, in terms of accuracy, from 70 to 100 yards, depending on the caliber, and ammunition used. The basic idea here is that many people living in an urban or suburban environment may not need any more additional range out of a weapon. At present, you would not want to use an assault rifle for

---

[5]   Since the first edition of this book, Smith & Wesson no longer manufacture this AR15 upper, likely due to a current import shortage of surplus 5.45mm ammunition from Russia.

home defense. Actually, you *can* use an assault rifle for home defense, if you're not worried about the bullet going through the bad guy at over 2000 fps, out of your house, and into the next three houses, all with innocent people inside of them.

Pistol carbines can also be a lot cheaper than buying a rifle, for those on a budget. There are conversion kits that allow you to convert a pistol that you already have, into a longer-barreled, short rifle. In addition, pistol ammunition tends to be cheaper than rifle ammo. I would recommend a pistol conversion such as the ones made by Mech-Tech Systems, out of Kalispell, Montana (http://www.mechtechsys.com/). They make carbine conversions for both Glocks, and M1911's. Their product is an accessory, not a main, serial-numbered weapons part, that falls under any federal regulations, etc (unless you live in California; they can't be shipped there). Just buy it on-line, and it comes to your door. Not only are you buying American, you are also buying from a well-established, and cute little "mom-and-pop" operation.

Some people have issues with using a pistol carbine as a main battle rifle (MBR). Jim Rawles is one of them. His primary concerns are the lower velocities that come from pistol cartridges, as compared to rifle cartridges. This basically equates to stopping power. Granted, if you lived on a ranch, where your nearest neighbor is a half-mile away, you should stick with an assault rifle, large-caliber bolt action rifle, etc

Mech Tech Systems carbine conversion for the Glock 17 9mm handgun, fully assembled. It is shown here with a 33-round Glock magazine, one-inch riser, holographic electronic sight, and a three-point sling. This type of sling is very useful for having both hands free for various tasks, while at the same time having the weapon at the ready. An ideal arrangement while doing paperwork, driving a vehicle, or riding a motorcycle.

However, years ago, after I had developed my own theory about pistol carbines for urban dwellers, the Army Special Forces–types and security contractors who were operating in places like Baghdad at the time, were picking the 9mm Beretta *Storm*, a dedicated 9mm carbine (not pistol conversion), in place of the 5.56mm M4 (the current military issue, shorter barrel version of the M16). Within 100 yards, its "knockdown" effect was much greater than that of a tiny little 55, or 60-grain .22 bullet moving through the bad guys at hyper speeds. Pistol carbines also allow you to shoot ammunition with a stronger powder charge, such as 9mm +P+, or .45 ACP +P, which would eventually damage a pistol, over time. A 9mm +P+ round out of a long barrel, at over 1400 fps., is roughly the equivalent of a .357 Magnum, or .30 cal. M-1 Carbine round moving downrange.

During the Vietnam War, US Army Special Forces soldiers began the special ops trend of being armed with an ammunition-paired sub-machinegun and pistol. For example, some would carry a 9mm British Sten sub-machinegun, in addition to a Browning Hi-Power pistol. Another pair would be a .45 ACP M3A1 "Grease gun" sub-machinegun, or the old gangster-era Thompson with stick magazines, and a standard-issue M1911 pistol.

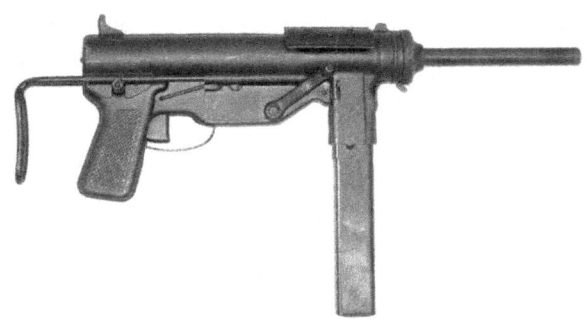

M3A1 sub-machinegun (Wikipedia)

In the case of the average urban Survivalist, this is where the beauty of a pistol carbine comes in: Versatility. For example, you can either carry an additional Glock pistol as a backup to a dedicated carbine, such as the Kel-Tec carbines which take Glock magazines, or with the proper amount of practice with a pistol conversion, convert quickly back into a pistol, from the carbine configuration (in the event of a weapons malfunction, damage to the conversion piece, the situational need to "dress down," etc). Extended barrel carbine conversions by themselves are easy to stow in backpacks, etc.

Avoid "carbine kits" that are basically just a dress-up kit that attaches *around* an existing pistol. These are just gimmicks, in my opinion, courtesy of the firearm accessories industry. (in other words, "Mall Ninjas of the World, Unite!"). While the ergonomics may improve one's accuracy, it does nothing to improve ballistics.

These designs remove the original benefits of having a pistol: Concealability and one-handed operation, in extremely close quarters. In addition, these conversions do not allow for the routine use of the hotter loadings of ammunition, previously described.

Going in the other direction, *avoid* rifles that are configured as pistols, such as the pistol AK's, or the pistol AR-15's (these AR-uppers are cheap for a reason). These are nothing but monstrosities, another product-idea gimmick made for the civilian gun market. When you put a rifle cartridge into a pistol, you end-up wasting a perfectly good cartridge. In an extremely short barrel, all you get is a massive amount of muzzle flash, with less range, and less accuracy. In other words, most of the cartridges' energy gets wasted as the bullet exits the barrel. The still-burning gasses will literally knock the bullet into another direction, as it leaves the barrel. For this reason, most public ranges actually *ban* these weapons from their facilities.

Pistol AK (Wikipedia)

In addition, although .22 LR is a good rifle *and* pistol cartridge, avoid shooting the hypervelocity cartridges (CCI Stinger, Aguila Supermaximum, etc.) out of a pistol. You will get the same effect, as mentioned above. The same goes for .22 Magnum, in particular, which is basically a .22 LR on steroids (small Derringers have actually been made in this caliber, if you can believe that!). Because of the newer generation of hypervelocity .22 LR ammunition, I believe that .22 Magnum is on its way to becoming less-and-less popular (CCI Stinger and Aguila Supermaximum actually have the same muzzle energy as .22 Magnum, anyway). Don't get me wrong: There is no problem in using a hypervelocity .22 in a pistol. The energy in the cartridge will definitely work the action on a .22 LR pistol conversion for your existing M1911 or Glock pistols (these .22 slide conversions have traditionally had problems with lower-powered .22 LR). However, just expect to have a lot of muzzle flash, and a lot less accuracy.

In conclusion, pistol carbines (both dedicated and pistol conversion) can be an effective weapon for the average urban/suburban survivalist, based on their effectiveness within 100 yards, cost, versatility, and ammunition compatibility.

d. Results from Tests Conducted with Hypervelocity .22LR

In April of 2007, I tested the three hottest "hypervelocity" .22 Long Rifle cartridges. Because of the easy storage, accuracy and effects of .22 ammunition at ranges out to 150 yards (not to mention the fun of shooting a customized Ruger 10/22), I've had a second love affair with the round, since being a child. It's the ultimate Survivalist cartridge.

These tests compared Aguila "Supermaximum," CCI Stinger and the full 40-grain CCI Velocitor. These tests were conducted at 100 yards, using a Ruger 10/22, customized with a 20" Butler Creek bull barrel on a floating Butler Creek lightweight bull barrel stock with Harris bipod, competition 1 oz. trigger, and polyurethane buffer pin. The scope is a Simmons 3-9x32. The spring weather was sunny, with a slight right-to-left wind in a mountainous area.

My first shots were three-round zeroing groups of the Mexican-made Aguila Ammo, a 30 grain slug with a screaming muzzle velocity of approximately 1,730 fps. Groups #1 and #3 measured 2 1/2 inches at their widest points, with groups #2 and #4 measuring 5" and 6" inches, respectfully. In other words, even out of a bull-barreled 10/22, these rounds were all over the place, although they were getting there very fast.

My next four groups were five-shot groups, alternating between CCI Stinger and CCI Velocitor for each two sets of groups. Group #1 for the Stinger ammo (1,650 fps) was down and to-the-left by two inches square, and two inches left and five inches down for the slower (1,435 fps) 40 gr. Velocitor round. Deciding at this point that I was going to relegate my stockpile of .22 Aguila to practice ammo, I began making zeroing adjustments based on my Stinger groups.

During the course of this, the Stinger five-round groups were 2 1/2" to 3", but remained consistent, with as many as three of the holes touching. The Velocitor groups measured 1 3/4" to 2", with three rounds in the last group all touching, and could fit in the area of a dime. The other two rounds in this group were high.

As for any other variables, I could probably have used a better scope. Second, I could have used a better barrel, as there are better barrel makers than Butler Creek (Volquartsen, Kidd Innovative Design, etc.) Also, being a runner, I have a strong heartbeat, which I can feel as I shoot, and probably need to train to shoot between heartbeats. The bottom line, however, is that I am now rotating through the Aguila ammo, then Stinger, and saving the 40-grain Velocitor for my SHTF/TEOTWAWKI/zeroing supply.

What I concluded from these tests was that CCI Velocitor is simply the most accurate, as well as destructive (due to its full 40-grain slug) .22 LR cartridge. Once you can acquire good accuracy with a good .22 round, think of it as a good remotely-operated brain surgery tool, if the need ever arises (which hopefully it won't).

Again, firearm ownership and deployment are varied, depending on the shooter, and the environment. Unless you are military or law enforcement experienced with firearms, you should seek-out training programs like The Appleseed Pro ect, The National Rifle Association, etc. The best schools are the ones run, or at least inspired by Vietnam Veterans, who spent their time (and training, beforehand) fighting from the prone position (on their stomachs), and behind some sort of cover, rather than depending on body armor.

Above all else, as I conclude this chapter: Safety is the most important aspect of firearm use. Otherwise, what's the point of being a survivalist?

- Assume that all weapons are loaded, as you encounter them.

- Never point a weapon at anyone, unless intending to use it.

- As you come within reach of another firearm, remove the magazine, then check the chamber for a chambered round. In the case of a revolver, pull the cylinder out, and inspect each chamber. In the case of older rifles with internal magazines, inspect that area, as well as the tube magazines in shotguns, etc. Besides, you'll look cool, demonstrating your firearms knowledge. Teach this knowledge to your children, as well.

XIV. Dealing with Refugees

As previously mentioned we could see human misery and suffering in the US, unlike anything we have seen since the American Civil War. Most people are not preppers, and for that reason, could be wandering aimlessly, along with other refugees, in the aftermath of a cataclysmic societal event. Some of these people who have heard about the preparedness, self-reliance, or survivalism cultures, may have already chosen the more sociopathic, coping mechanism, by having already stated, "I don't need to prep. I have a weapon, and I just need to know who all the other preppers are."

This is an important chapter, because many within the preparedness movement are not psychologically prepared to deal with refugees, or people coming to your door, to beg for food, or work, in the midst of a societal collapse.

In the case of the latter, The Depression era was known for people going door-to-door, looking for work. However, in the present day, opening the door for everyone who shows up is not a good idea. Just ask those poor, adopted, disabled kids, in Beulah, Florida, who in 2009 saw their parents murdered, in a military-style raid on their property, which was even planned by an active duty military member who belonged to US Special Operations Command, who was part of the gang. Some of these people were originally hired by the parents to do repair/remodeling work, and were allowed repeatedly into the house.

You need to analyze your area, and determine your situation: Urban, suburban, or rural, and the potential event, in order of the most likely:

In suburbia, we all live near major "lines of drift." In other words, major freeways, boulevards, and avenues. In the event of a major societal event, these are the trails that refugees will travel along.

If your neighborhood has not formed a community by this time, with established security, to include roadblocks and checkpoints, then your only recourse will be to operate on your own, with whoever you have for people living at your home. Ironically, you may have been fortunate enough, due to hard economic times, to have "doubled-up." In other words, you now have your own grown children, and maybe even Grandpa, living with you. The more numbers in a household, the more people to run around-the clock security with.

Initially, you may have people begging at your door. There is an additional dilemma here, however. Many in the preparedness community, particularly those motivated by religious convictions, may feel obliged to dispense charity. This can be done tactically. However, if you are not in a position to do this, then you should not open the door, *period*. Remember: If you are going to "bug in," then you want to hide in plain sight. If anything, you wi l want to appear poor and needy, yourself. When people show up, asking for food, fuel, etc., you should respond (through a window) in a weak, sickly voice, "We don't have any."

In the present world, if you have conversations with the neighbors, you need to watch what you say, depending on the types of people you have for neighbors. If they are the NFL / NASCAR / Disneyland types previously mentioned, NEVER mention your preps, or bring anything up about the collapse of industrial civilization. If someone else brings-up any concerns about US Government bankruptcy, the economy, the price of oil, etc., then *pretend that you are one of them*, by replying with statements such as: "Oh, I think things will improve," or "I think this is just short-term," or "Oh, I'm not worried about that, etc." Remember: You do not owe these people any favors. Don't try to be a do-gooder, for their sake. These people have had just as much opportunity as you to do their own research, learn about how this world really works, and prepare for it. If they're not willing to be unplugged from *The Matrix*, then screw them, as far as I'm concerned.

The best example I can think of in dealing with the neighbors at present is from the CBS TV series *Jericho*. I loved that series, and think it was a great idea for CBS to put out a TV series that was literally made by, and for survivalists (granted, there was some obvious Hollywood in it). The character of Hawkins was an outright bad ass, who chose to live in the town of Jericho, in order to seek refuge for his estranged family somewhere in the central United States; before the nukes went off (he was somehow involved in the conspiracy to detonate the nuclear weapons). He was constantly being bugged by this chubby, little sheriff's deputy, Jimmy, who was suspicious (for other, more minor reasons), and was constantly visiting Hawkins at his house. It was the most irritating part of the entire TV series! However (more than I would have been able to), Hawkins maintained himself, and stayed polite to Jimmy, throughout, since Hawkins was actually a good guy, whose intention was to assimilate his family into the community and help it out, in order to ensure mutual survival (not to mention that he had one of the nuclear devices in his possession, as proof of a plot by a certain government contractor to overthrow the government of the United States).

If, unfortunately, your status as a survivalist is blown, the neighbors previously mentioned will be at your doorstep, probably with their kids in tow, firstly asking if they can "borrow" some food items, toiletries, etc. Then they will bug you, offering to do work for you, in return for feeding their family. Then, they will likely get with other neighbors, and figure out how to forcibly confront you, in order to enter your home and take what they want.

In this described scenario, some preppers are actually prepping in order to help-out, if not outright distribute food and other supplies to their un-prepared neighbors. Well, if you're fairly well-off to rich, and feel like a philanthropist, then more power to you. It might even be the icebreaker that helps to form a cohesive community. However, most of us are not capable of such charity. Jim Rawles at Survivalblog.com has repeatedly mentioned in interviews that "I don't see my food storage as a three-year supply for one family. I see it as a one-year supply for three families."

Here's my variation of this theme: I see my three-year food supply as *my* family's three year food supply, and everybody else can kiss my ass (Except for certain individuals who already have an open invite, based on their skill-sets and overall personality, provided they bring as much of their own stuff as possible). Based on where I live, I am not in a position to dispense charity, as many others will not be (No offense, Jim. I think you understand).

If we have a severe event, something along the lines of the books *Patriots: A Novel of Survival in the Coming Collapse*, or *One Second After* (or Cormac McCarthy's *The Road*, for that matter), then people knocking on your door may get desperate, even when you have convincingly told them that you don't have anything to give.

Example: A male adult, after already been told "no," insists on coming in your house, anyway. He even has a group of people standing behind him on the sidewalk, which may even include women and children. He uses his shoulder on the door, trying to break in. He then calls his other male companions over to help knock the door in.

Immediately: Grab your home defense weapon (preferably a semi-automatic .12 gauge shotgun), and RUN to where your designated area is to cover your front door, with weapons fire. This can be a window in the front of the house with the window screen removed, a garage window, or if you have enough land in front of your house, a family member / friend already outside, on LP/OP duty. At this time, cycle a round into the chamber, aim at the leader of the groups' head, and pull the trigger. However, based on the actual threat, your ammo use may vary.

To kill the leader of a group of people with ill intent, during a period without any rule of law is a good thing. For the people within said group to suddenly see their leaders' head explode: *Priceless*. People will usually leave your property at that point. Plus, a headless body (or two) left on your doorstep makes a pretty good deterrent. Any evil- doers walking around your neighborhood will probably say to themselves "Well, scratch that house off, boys." During a period of relative calm, you can later, and carefully, search the body (or bodies) for intelligence: Where did they come from? Where were they heading? What information have they collected? What weapons and tools are they using, etc.

The resolution described in this example may sound barbaric, and medieval. However, this is exactly the type of scenario that we need to psychologically prepare ourselves for.

Another possibility is a continual line of refugees, passing in front of your house. You may have to actually stand out there with your weapon and body armor on, telling people, "Move along, move along, there's nothing here for you."

A good coping mechanism to use is to remember the simple fact that these people were probably still living in their NFL/NASCAR/Disneyland state-of-mind, when things progressed to this point. They were probably the type that even laughed at people within the preparedness movement. The fact that you were able to foresee possible events years earlier, and plan for them, gives meaning to the term "survival of the fittest." In my case, I grew up with no capital of any type: Social (family) or material (money, wealth, etc), and despite all this, made a life for myself. As an adult, knowing what I knew about human nature from my own experiences, I planned ahead. Why couldn't these people have prepped, who began their lives with much more in resources than I ever had?

Hopefully this chapter has given the reader a "wake-up call," as to what we will have to mentally prepare for, regarding the less fortunate. We need to remember that at all levels, human beings in our current culture feed on human weakness (why do you think that the US invaded Iraq in 2003? After all, their military had never recovered from the first Gulf War). This ties in with what was previously covered in the previous chapter on mental attitude. Remember: We are in a state of socio-economic collapse *right now.* Personally, I have already been in situations myself that mirror the situations from an apocalyptic movie, or computer role-playing game (RPG).

For instance, at my regular automotive shop, an older, overweight guy with a cane came into the shop, complaining that one of the mechanics used his truck for personal business (the mechanic *had* actually used the guy's truck to transport an engine. How the customer found-out, I have no idea). While this older disabled guy was requesting that the mechanic be fired, and was threatening a lawsuit against the shop, through the front of the shop I noticed at least one younger person in the truck he arrived in, who looked ready for action. While this fat piece of crap was trying to get out of paying for the service that was performed on his vehicle (and the service was completed on his vehicle), that was when I began sticking up for the mechanics. I noticed the guy in the truck outside staring at me. The mechanic honored this dirt bag's request, and did not charge him.

Looking back on that scenario, I wish I had done more to stick up for these guys, insisting that he pay the shop for said services, and that the ass clown that he had brought with him for muscle had better stay in his vehicle.

Standing up for yourself or other people like this can be scary, as you are dealing with the unknown. However, we need to work through these fears, and start learning how to take a punch, literally. This is why many gangs have timed (and *somewhat* controlled) physical group beatings of a person, as an "initiation." Everyone fears the hell out of this type of situation. However, once the initiate experiences this, he learns that it was not only survivable, but that he *really can* take a punch. Many of the best martial arts schools also use light sparing in their training (after a waiver of liability is signed, of course), meaning that especially if the two sparring individuals know each other, and happen to be aggressive, that there will be bruises, and possibly injuries.

Sometimes, particularly as I write something like this, I get choked-up, remembering our old large, solid black, muscular cat, Blackjack, who I nick-named "Macho," or "Macho Kitty," as my wife called him. He had been part of a litter, that lost its mother, and he had been brutalized by the experience. He was not a very friendly cat; with a face that sometimes reminded me of Godzilla (I had wondered at one time why we even kept him. However, just like human beings tend to do, he did mellow-out in his later years). He was like a feline version of Mr. T, of *The A Team* and *Rocky III* fame. That cat did not sweat anybody or anything. Even in his older years, any large dog that came into our yard, he would stare them down, and actually jump up into the air, and attack them! He gave religion to any dogs that even thought of messing with him. He was the bravest cat I ever knew.

I think we all have something to learn from other mammals, even cats.

XV Camouflage and Concealment

Camouflage is basically the art and science of not getting noticed by the human minds-eye. As preppers and survivalists, 90 % of our efforts should be focused on simply not being noticed, whether we live in the city, on a farm, or in the woods. All the tactical weapons training in the world, from places like Front Sight, Thunder Ranch, etc. will be of no use, if 50 violent, and heavily armed starving refugees discover your family, living at your food-producing doomstead, outside the city. At that point, you better have a massive amount of firepower on your side, and expect to take casualties.

As survivalists, we are not always trying to achieve complete concealment. But at all times, we are basically messing with the human mind's eye. In other words, even if a person *does* physically see something, it may not register *consciously* with them.

Here is one example: In an article posted at SurvivalBlog.com a few years ago (and reprinted in this book), one gentleman was describing his adventures during the societal collapse environment created in the aftermath of Hurricane Katrina. While parked at a certain location around other cars and people, this man noticed an agitated person going from car-to-car, offering to buy any spare gasoline they may have had with them. The person who provided this article wrote that when this man approached him, it was because he visibly saw the fuel cans in the bed of his pickup. As this clown was turned-down in his attempt to buy this gentleman's fuel, he then insisted that he was just going to take it, because it was an emergency, and that he had to get home. At that point, the driver of the truck introduced this retard to Mr. 1911 (his M1911 .45 pistol), at which time the dirtbag went away.

The takeaway that this gentleman had from this event was

that he should have had a tarp covering everything he had in the bed in his truck. I can think of one better: That next time he uses an earth-tone tarp, in either green, or brown, that are becoming more popular among homeowners, soccer moms, etc., who want something that will blend into their yards better, than the usual, podunk-looking blue tarp (blue is a bad color, as it is not an earth-tone. We'll discuss this more in detail).

Whether it is concealing yourself in the woods, or dressing a certain way in the urban environment, all camouflage concepts are the same. The following images are taken from what I believe is the best book ever written on the subject: The US Army's FM (Field Manual) 5-20: *Camouflage*, printed in 1968.

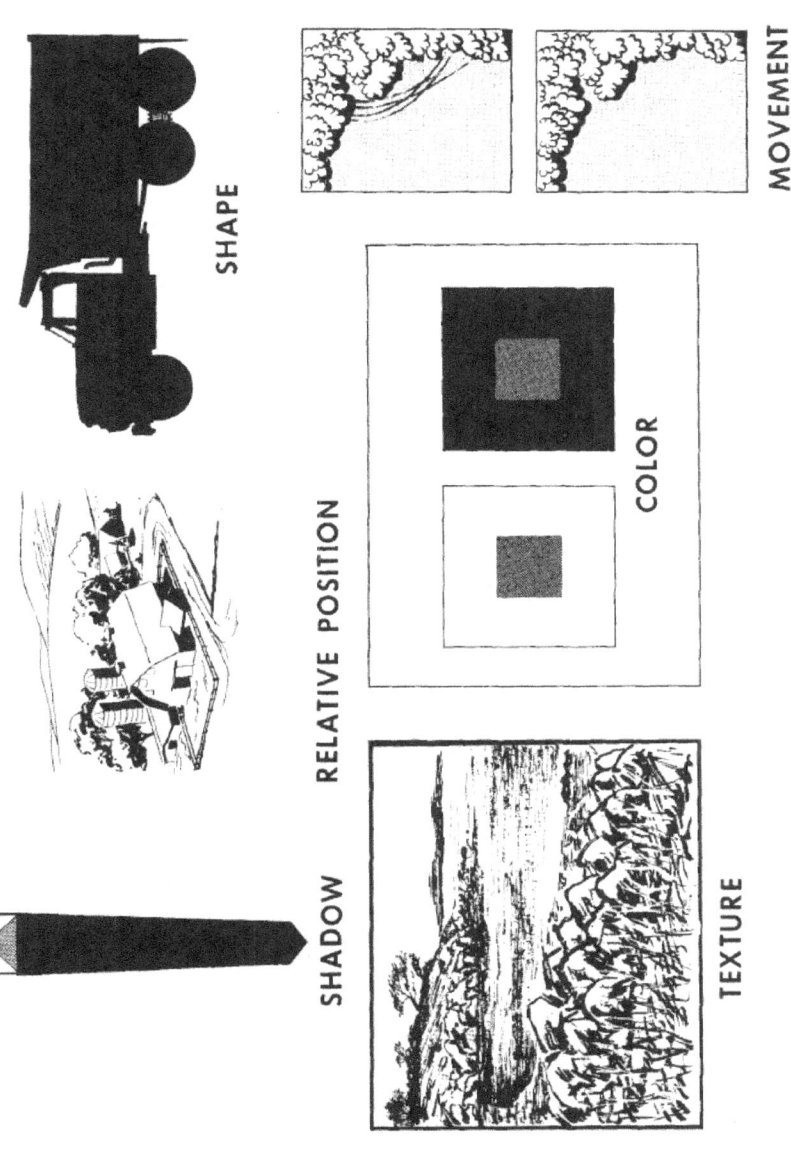

SHAPE

RELATIVE POSITION

SHADOW

MOVEMENT

COLOR

TEXTURE

Figure 8. Factors of recognition.

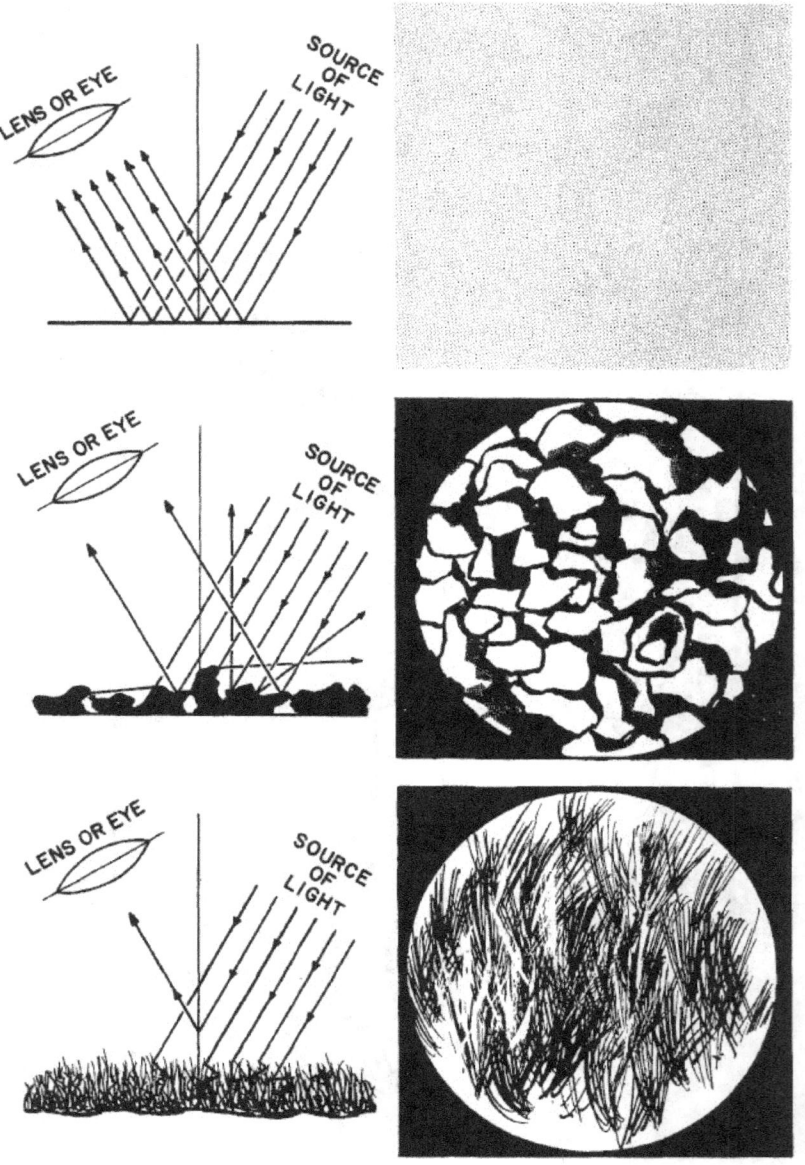

Figure 9. How texture influences dark and light appearance.

From the two preceding images, we can see how movement, shadow, texture, relative position, color, and reflected light from an object all affect the mind's eye. These are based on basic laws of physics, which I do not believe have changed much, since 1968.

During the writing of this book, it was revealed, however, why the US Army leadership did not practice what the Army preached, regarding these concepts, when they came-up with the horribly non-inclusive Army Combat Uniform, or ACU. According to the article "$5B CAMO SNAFU: Army Ditches Failed Combat Uniform That Put a Target on Grunts' Backs for 8 Years," the civilian scientists at the US Army's Research Center in Natick, Massachusetts were however, using these concepts when working on a digital pattern for the Army, based on the US Marine Corps lead, when the Marine Corps developed the MARPAT digital camouflage pattern, back in 2002. The problem was apparently political:

> The fact that the government spent $5 billion on a camouflage design that actually made its soldiers more visible — and then took eight years to correct the problem — has also left people in the camouflage industry incensed. The total cost comes from the Army itself and includes the price of developing the pattern and producing it for the entire service branch.
>
> ... The problem, the researchers said, was an oddly named branch of the Army in charge of equipping soldiers with gear — Program Executive Office Soldier — had suddenly ordered Natick's camouflage team to pick a pattern long before trials were finished.
>
> "They jumped the gun," said James Fairneny, an electrical engineer on Natick's camouflage team.
>
> Researchers said they received a puzzling order: Take the winning colors and create a pixilated

pattern. Researchers were ordered to "basically put it in the Marine Corps pattern," Fairneny said.

For a decision that could ultimately affect more than a million soldiers in the Army, reserves and National Guard, the sudden shift from Program Executive Office Soldier was a head-scratcher. The consensus among the researchers was the Army brass had watched the Marine Corps don their new uniforms and caught a case of pixilated camouflage envy.

"It was trendy," Stewardson said. "If it's good enough for the Marines, why shouldn't the Army have that same cool new look?"

The brigadier general ultimately responsible for the decision, James Moran, who retired from the Army after leaving Program Executive Office Soldier, has not responded to messages seeking comment.

It's worth noting that, flawed as it was, the universal pattern did solve the problem of mismatched gear, said Eric Graves, editor of the military gear publication Soldier Systems Daily, adding that the pattern also gave soldiers a new-looking uniform that clearly identified the Army brand.

"Brand identity trumped camouflage utility," Graves said. "That's what this really comes down to: 'We can't allow the Marine Corps to look more cool than the Army.' "

This uniform color pattern was originally marketed as an "all-inclusive uniform," which falsely suggested that this uniform was intended for all environments: Woodlands, deserts, jungles, etc. It is obvious that the colors were picked for their ability to counter night vision devices, due to the mix of light greens and grays, which are difficult to see through light-amplification night vision devices (Other than that, I will admit that the pattern seems to work in colorless urban areas, but that is about it).

If I had any say over it, I would have saved the Army billions, and simply gone back to the original single-color Vietnam-era olive drab (OD) green jungle fatigue concept, but in the more modern (and proven) lightweight Battle Dress Uniform (BDU) design. Having spoken to some local law enforcement about the effectiveness of solid earth-tone colored BDU's, and seeing video of various SWAT teams in action, I notice that this is exactly what many departments are currently wearing.

The reason as to why I included this snafu regarding the Army ACU pattern is because it is a sign of the times that we currently live in (not just because I happen to be an Army dog): Diminishing returns on complexity (Tainter). One man was ultimately responsible (BG Moran) for the worst camouflage pattern in US Army history, because of "digital camo envy." This reminds me of why I kept my service to the Army (as a reservist) at arms-length, since 9/11. Being a historian of empire: I was not going to be a pawn of these idiots at the top.

One particular topic that I will be focusing on in this chapter is the countering of aerial, or overhead imagery from...yes, you guessed it: Drones. As mentioned elsewhere in this book, it has been a slippery slope on the part of the powers-that-be, and particularly the current US president to go from using drones to spot targets for manned attack, to armed drones doing the job themselves on individually targeted people in Pakistan (with the overwhelming number of deaths being innocent civilians), to the targeting of people in Yemen, which has included US Citizens, without any due process whatsoever.

The last time that I checked, one of the best things about being a US Citizen is that we are supposed to have inalienable rights, such as that of due process, and the right to be judged by our peers (Our rights under the US Constitution, at least before anyone systematically kills us, anyway). After that comes extended unemployment benefits, cheap prices on grocery items and free Wi-Fi (in other words, if you travel around this world, you will see that people in other various countries actually have more personal freedoms, civil protections, etc. than we do, while we are constantly bombarded with propaganda in the US about how "free" we are, and that our military is currently fighting for those freedoms).

As of this writing, there has been the discovery of a "kill list," overseen by President Obama himself, with the help of two-dozen advisors, who meet on a regular basis. The individuals on this list brought to Obama included a 17 year-old girl, living inside the US (a 16-year-old male was targeted and killed, along with his 12-year old cousin in December, 2011, simply because he was *planning* on video-documenting the aftermaths of the drone strikes in Pakistan, and had nothing to do with militant Islam), *and other US Citizens*.

The 2010 novel *American Apocalypse II: Refuge* describes a period of time starting a few years from now, where as things begin to really fall apart, the US Government uses armed drones against its perceived enemies, who happen to be US citizens, *within* the US. This is just another example of how authors who have recently written either dystopic, or apocalyptic fiction have had to re-write scenes within their novels, as some of their future events have become fact, before their works were even finished.

Again, fiction has a strange way of becoming future fact...

α. Urban

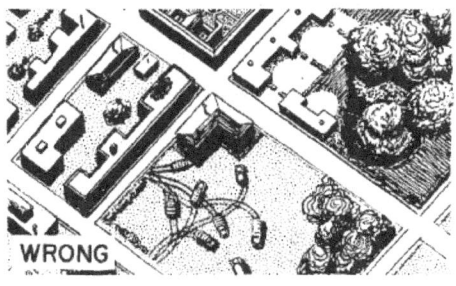

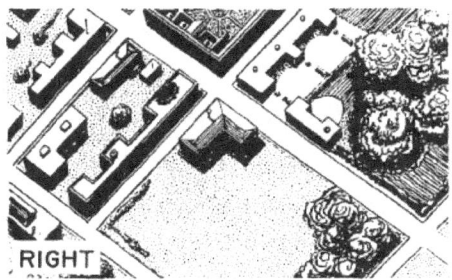

Figure 13. *In regular urban terrain, military objects must be sited parallel to and close to pattern lines.*

In the urban environment, we want to maintain straight lines. One must understand that in nature, THERE ARE NO STRAIGHT LINES. In the urban and suburban environments (to a high degree, at least), however, EVERYTHING IS IN STRAIGHT LINES. Therefore, in the urban environment, do not interfere with already existing streets, roads, sidewalks, paved walkways, etc. Vehicular discipline is imperative when you have vehicles operating on your property, or in your operational area. Do not let anyone take shortcuts across fields, lawns, unpaved areas, etc. Rope these areas off with signs attached, if necessary.

b. Suburban

Thanks to the existence of parasitic land developers, many

cities have grown out, not up. This has created sprawl, that consists of large surface streets, suburbs, and retail crap that seems to stretch-on forever, rarely higher than two or three-story structures. Many survivalists who end-up in an emergency situation in this environment are either going to be hunkering down, hidden in plain sight, or traveling through this terrain.

If hunkering down, depending on the situation, you will need to address every aspect of blending in: BS'ing the neighbors, physical state of your yard / house, and good old light and noise discipline, in the event of a power-down scenario.

We'll start with the neighbors; in the present (hopefully society hasn't already collapsed completely, as of the publishing of this book). This depends on who your neighbors are, and how close to them you actually live.

If you live in suburbia, particularly upper-middle class on-up, your neighbors probably already live within the dominant culture, meaning NFL, NASCAR and Disneyland. Do you already know your neighbors, and get along with them? If you do, then that's a good thing.

If you know your neighbors, and they share the same beliefs as you do regarding the future (to include the entire spectrum from progressive eco-happy doomers, to fellow survivalists, etc), then this is great! However, most neighborhoods are not as blessed.

If you are a prepper / survivalist in a typical neighborhood of NFL / NASCAR and you do not have much in common with your neighbors, then you need to use deception. In other words, instead of having a reputation as the neighborhood camouflage-clad weirdo (hopefully this has not already happened), or someone with shortwave and UHF antennas all over your property, the outside of your house and your personal attire needs to match that of everyone else's.

If you need a new roof on your house for instance, don't go looking for a fireproof steel one (although that's the type that all of us survivalists would love to have), when all the other houses in the neighborhood use regular shingled roofs. For doors, widows, etc., depending on your budget, at least make sure that they have a façade that *looks* like a normal residential door.

In addition, *everything* in and around your yard should be in earth tones. Instead of the usual blue colored tarps and bright orange or yellow-colored electrical extension cords, make sure that everything you use outside of your house is colored in shades of green, brown, or tan, depending on the region you live in. These earth-tone colored items are easy to find at all the big box stores. Also, avoid tarps, etc. in camouflage patterns. As previously mentioned, camouflage patterns in themselves will draw attention, as compared to solid earth-tone colors. In anything but a purely tactical environment, they will stick-out. Make sure you position these everyday items based on what this chapter describes, with regards to straight lines, shadow, overhead concealability, etc.

For clothing, earth-tones are the best for all environments, including urban (take a look sometime. What colors are many downtown buildings painted in?). Try to avoid constant wear of anything camouflage, unless it is currently in style, such as the cargo-pocket shorts in military camouflage that everyone seems to wear in summer, with an un-tucked shirt. Although I have the same love/hate thing with Wal-Mart as everyone else does, I have noticed within the last two years that they seem to have a very good line of inexpensive, earth-tone clothing, to include OD green long-sleeve pullover shirts, and camouflage trousers (with cargo pockets) that are in shades of light green and brown (with no black color in the mix), made by Wrangler. These trousers are very common, due to their price. Unfortunately, they seem shaped in an almost bell-bottom, straight leg design. My wife managed to re-stitch these, into regular military-style trouser legs.

(Wikipedia)

In our clothing, vehicles, equipment, etc, we want to avoid the use of bright, non-earth tone colors: Blues, reds, etc. Particularly black, which despite being used in many camo patterns, is not a natural color. In the above image, this person is being viewed in the near infrared (near IR), wearing the US military's standard 1980's to early 2000's Battle Dress Uniform. Notice how everything black sticks out like a sore thumb: The rifle, his boots, and all of the black in his clothing. With the proliferation of night vision devices using this portion of the light frequency spectrum, we need to remember that our normal eyesight represents only a very narrow region within the light portion of the energy spectrum.

If things do get as bad as in a "lights-out" scenario, then you also want to be prepared for that event, if your town, the region you live in, or the whole Northern Hemisphere for some reason loses electrical power. You want to appear as dark as everyone else in the neighborhood. If you hook up your super-dooper alternative energy system, complete with a wind generator and solar panels, and your house is lit in the evenings as if nothing ever happened, then you are going to draw attention, and visitors. Needless to say, depending on the length of the power outage, depending solely on a fuel-run generator is outright idiotic for a suburban survivalist, for many reasons. Priority should be to learn to live without an electrical generator, as a foundation for self-reliant living.

I actually have my own experience in this area, from a similar event. Back in my early 20's when I was eager to own my own property, I owned a mobile home with a propane tank for our furnace, water heater and stove. My family at that time experienced a power outage during a winter storm. That evening, we heard a knock on the door. It was the overweight female neighbor, from next door, within the mobile home park. She asked if we could warm-up her baby's formula bottle, which we were glad to do. After we noticed her staying outside while we did this for her, we did the right thing, and invited her in, out of the cold. We had a pleasant conversation, and we were glad to have helped-out, and offered to continue assisting her while the storm continued. Although we really did not know her (and really didn't want to know her initially, due to the other people that seemed to live there), she turned out to be a very nice person. We were happy to help, as it was a temporary mini-disaster, which resolved itself the next day.

However, the take-away from this was that I had a propane tank that was clearly visible. In a more desperate situation, we could have ended-up with a line of neighbors in front of our door, wanting us to cook their food, heat water for them, etc. Off-grid resources like these should *at least* be obscured with anything on hand, such as a tarp (earth-tone, of course), yard debris, etc.

Remember: Camouflage is a creative and artistic process, so be creative!

During a severe societal event involving an extended power outage, you want to practice what the military calls *light discipline*. Particularly if you are generating any light inside of your house from any hidden alternative energy sources, such as a small, quiet generator, etc (in other words anything other than candles). You will want to blackout your windows from inside, as much as possible, using blankets, garbage bags, etc. You should also have a dedicated "lightlock": A room in your house with an outside door that is *always* kept dark, that you use to enter and exit the house from at night. Think of it in terms of an airlock on a spacecraft, or a submarine, for example. Virtually all portable military structures have this sort of feature. A good way to confirm your level of light discipline is to go outside at night, using your natural night adjusted vision, or a night vision device, to look for any light leaks under doors, etc. Just this measure alone can go a long way to convince your neighbors that you don't have any special preps that they don't have, or that no one is living there, in the midst of other abandoned homes.

c. Rural

If you are already in a rural or semi-rural area with like-minded neighbors, this is like a dream come true! You can have regular meetings where individual skills and resources for the immediate community can be coordinated, barter relationships formed, etc. This is in addition to planning everything from a neighborhood watch on steroids (to coin the phrase from Jim Rawles), to tactical defensive plans, establishing sectors / fields of fire, logistics, etc. Again, the following images (with the exception of my own) are from US Army FM 5-20, *Camouflage*.

1 WRONG

2 RIGHT

Figure 10.   Choice of position.

In the above photo, this person is conducting a camouflage experiment, using a simple woodland-pattern US gov't-issue poncho, a pair of dark brown 99-cent work gloves, and a multi-use OD green triangular bandage to blend in with the adjacent foliage. Although the image seems bright, the light is coming from the camera's flash. This individual is well within the shadow of this temperate rain forest canopy. He is not only using the tree for ballistic protection (cover), but actually positioned himself into a small depression, almost like a small foxhole (site selection). He is aiming a highly-accurized, customized 10/22 rifle (in .22 LR) at a dirt road, about 30 yards away. The only deficiency spotted here is the all-black rifle, itself: No camouflage has been applied to it, in the form of strips of burlap, a Duracoat paintjob, or any other weapons camouflaging product (remember: black is not a natural color). Also, his cotton work gloves make good infantryman gloves, but here they should be a lighter brown, or green in color (such as Nomex pilot gloves, etc).

This is a straight-on photo of the individual shown above, or at least in his direction, from the road that the shooter is aiming at. It is impossible to see him, but the shooter has a clear view of the road. Again, this is only at about 20 yards. Does this mean that with the right hypervelocity .22 LR ammunition (i.e., CCI Stinger), that this person could throw an effective ambush, even against a heavily body-armored professional para-military force (using face, head and neck shots)? You bet! Philippine guerillas during WW II were known for impressive ambushes, performing head-shots with nothing other than single-shot .22 LR bolt-action rifles.

Figure 11. Example of proper siting and dispersal of tents in sparsely vegetated terrain (barren).

If you ever have to evacuate an urban area with all of your goodies (beans, bullets and band-aids), and you get to your own privately-owned land, or just decide to squat, this is how you want to position your camp (above, right). The best way to position a campsite based on shadow is to see where the sun is, based on the time of day. In the Northern Hemisphere, if you are standing, facing the sun at 12 Noon, then you know you are facing directly south, and that the sun will continue to travel towards your right (to the west), until it sets. Set-up your temporary (or permanent, for that matter) camps where you think the shadow will be at about 1-2 PM, depending on the season of the year, your latitude, etc.[6]

---

[6] As the sun travels through space, it actually wobbles, creating our four seasons, affecting length of day, and how high the sun travels through the sky, over the horizon. In addition, learn how to determine north/south using a watch (even a digital one will work: Just imagine where the hour hand would be). Also learn the stars: The Big Dipper, and the North Star (Polaris) in particular. I have been amazed at how people, of whom I have asked directions have been completely unable to determine north, when even standing next to an interstate that is following true north/south! Learn these basics of Earth's physics. Better yet, start teaching your children these skills. Just another reason why I agree with others that we are heading towards a human die-off (in the US, in particular), this century.

WRONG   RIGHT

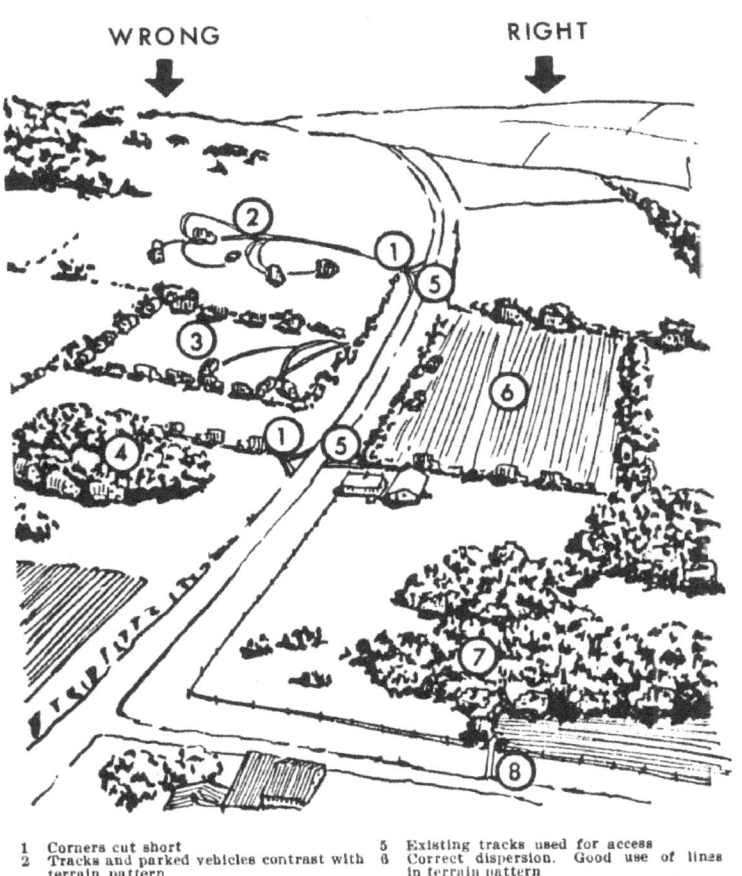

1	Corners cut short	5	Existing tracks used for access
2	Tracks and parked vehicles contrast with terrain pattern	6	Correct dispersion. Good use of lines in terrain pattern
3	Insufficient dispersion and exposed tracks of three vehicles	7	Correct dispersion and good use of overhead cover
4	Insufficient dispersion; newly made tracks point to position	8	Inconspicuous tracks to cultivated field

The above image is crucial information for a planned community, or neighborhood that wants to stay tactical. The key take-away here is that if you have an extensive piece of property, with other members of your group showing up with their vehicles, then *vehicular discipline must be emphasized*. This also applies to recently purchased pieces of rural property: Even years-old tire tracks left in fields, etc will continue to stick-out in overhead imagery, as if they were recently made. Use metal rakes, shovels, etc. to remove these old tire tracks!

Figure 16. It is obvious here, to even the untrained observer, that some activity is taking place at both ① and ② and bears watching.

Another example of a complete lack of vehicular discipline.

(1) Rubber bands, or expedient bands made from old inner tubes or burlap strips, secure natural materials. (Note position of band.)

(4) Texturing diminishes shine from steel helmet.

(2) Slits in burlap allow insertion of natural material.

(5) Burlap helmet cover pattern painted to break up solid color before natural materials are inserted.

(3) Form disrupted by burlap bows tied into slitted cover.

(6) A disruptive paint pattern, with the pattern carried across the curved lines of the edges, especially those seen from the front.

Figure 21. Various techniques for camouflaging the helmet.

Although the helmets pictured here are the good old USGI steel pot, the same camouflage can be applied to the more modern Kevlar helmets. As in these images, make sure the foliage is close to the helmet itself, and not sticking up a foot in the air. Remember: The human eye keys on movement.

Figure 22.   Shiny and bright skin must be toned down.

M-60 MACHINE GUN WRAPPED WITH CLOTH

RIFLE PATTERN PAINTED

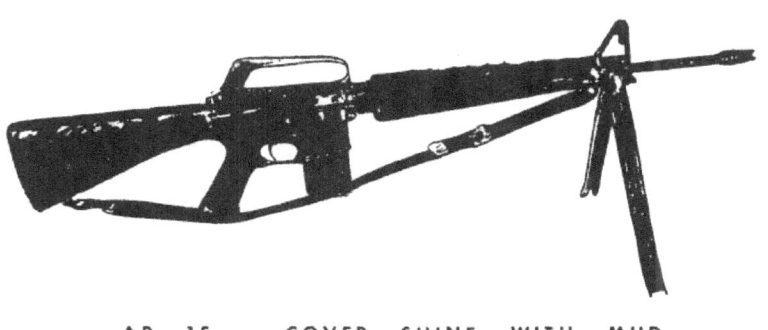

AR 15 - COVER SHINE WITH MUD

Figure 23. Suggestions for camouflaging an individual weapon.

These are the older, traditional methods for camouflaging a weapon. The more modern versions of this are epoxy-based paint jobs, such as DuraCoat, and self-adhesive cloth wraps, in various colors and camouflage patterns. Strips of burlap are also a good traditional form of individual weapon camouflage. They can be found in both traditional light brown and green colors at fabric stores, etc.

Figure 31. Throw the shadow onto something irregular.

If you cannot park a vehicle, or piece of equipment inside of shadow, then you need to hide the shadow of the vehicle itself. As humans (like all mammals), we readily identify objects based on their shadow, whether we see the object itself, or not.

The characteristic black shadow in the open end of a cargo truck can be seen for a considerable distance. One way to conceal this shadow is to drop the rear tarpaulin, another way is to use natural materials, as shown here.

Figure 33. Further measures to conceal vehicle.

Although the above example refers to a military vehicle (a good old "Deuce-and-a-half" in this case), the same applies to pickups with canopies, SUV's, etc. Keep those canopy hatches and rear doors closed!

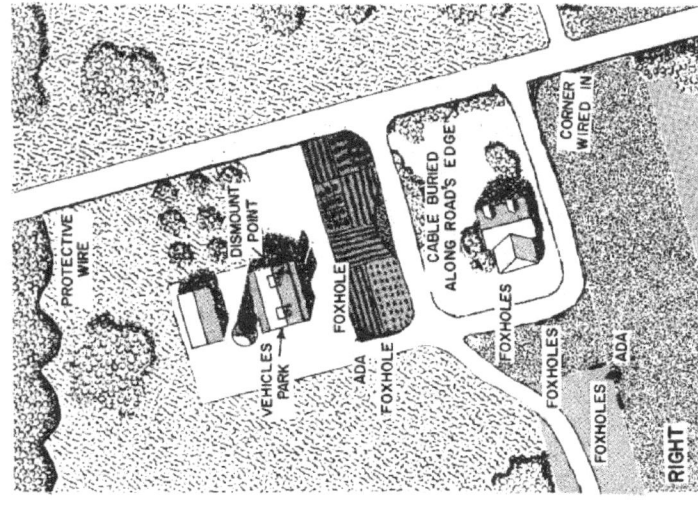

Labels (right image): PROTECTIVE WIRE, DISMOUNT POINT, VEHICLES PARK, FOXHOLE, ADA, FOXHOLE, CABLE BURIED ALONG ROAD'S EDGE, FOXHOLES, FOXHOLES, FOXHOLES, ADA, CORNER WIRED IN

THERE IS NOTHING IN THIS RURAL SCENE TO AROUSE SUSPICION. SUCH A CONTROLLED CP IS POSSIBLE ONLY IF A CAMOUFLAGE PLAN HAS BEEN MADE IN ADVANCE OF OCCUPATION AND FOLLOWED CLOSELY. MOST VEHICLES SHOULD BE PARKED UNDER COVER AT A DISTANCE FROM THE CP PERSONNEL SHOULD PROCEED ON FOOT TO THE BUILDING ITSELF. PROTECTIVE WIRE FOLLOWS TERRAIN LINES.

RIGHT

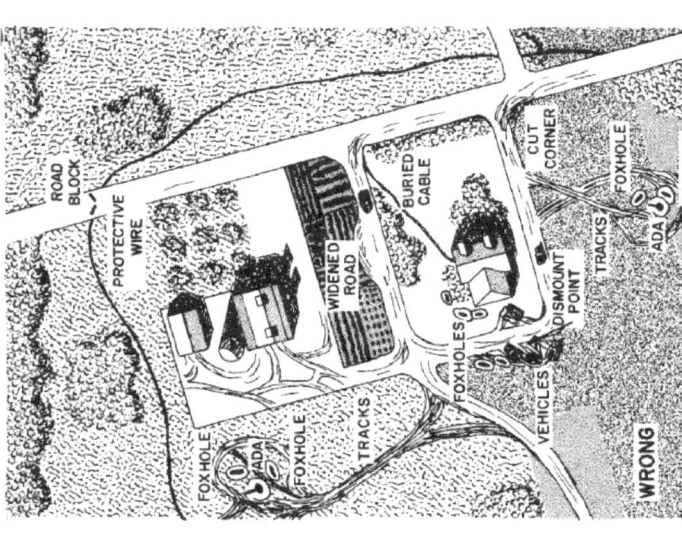

Labels (wrong image): ROAD BLOCK, PROTECTIVE WIRE, WIDENED ROAD, BURIED CABLE, CUT CORNER, FOXHOLE, FOXHOLES, DISMOUNT POINT, TRACKS, VEHICLES, ADA, FOXHOLE, TRACKS, FOXHOLE, ADA, FOXHOLE

EVEN A HASTY GLANCE AT THIS SCENE WOULD TELL THE ENEMY OBSERVER THAT THIS IS A COMMAND POST. ALL THE TELLTALE SIGNS ARE THERE. THEY ARE MILITARY MARKS ON AN OTHERWISE ORDINARY RURAL SCENE.

WRONG

Figure 48. Layout of a command post.

158

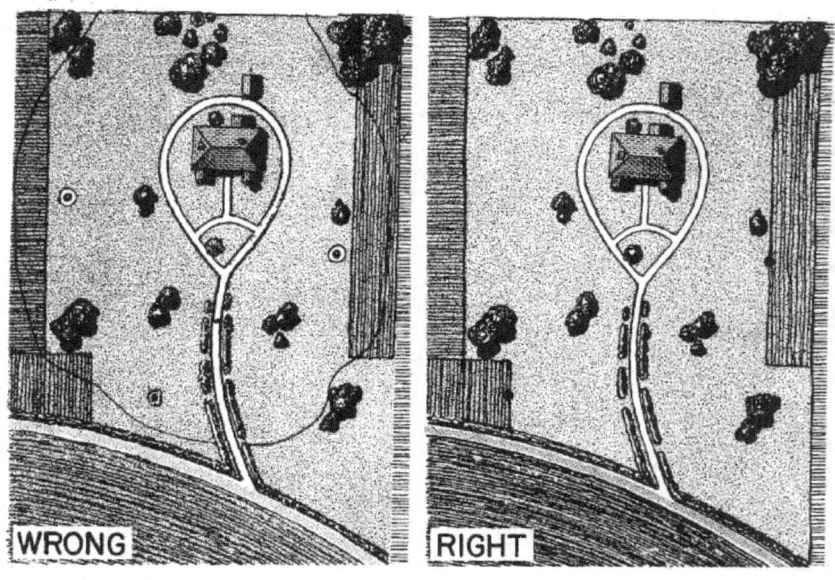

WRONG

RIGHT

Figure 47. Proper layout of protective wire.

The above image shows a house (or potential retreat compound) that is lucky enough to have deployed some protective wire. Again, in the age of aerial drones and public-domain satellite imagery, we want to conceal the deployment of any barbed wire, razor wire, concertina, etc. from overhead view, if possible. Remember: In the world of man-made environments, we want to think in terms of straight lines. Obviously, the above example requires much more wire to achieve this effect. However, concealability *is the priority*. If you have a limited amount of wire, then prioritize its deployment based on likely avenues of approach, other natural obstacles, etc., with the thought of canalizing (channelizing) the threat into observable areas, early-warning devices, booby traps, etc.

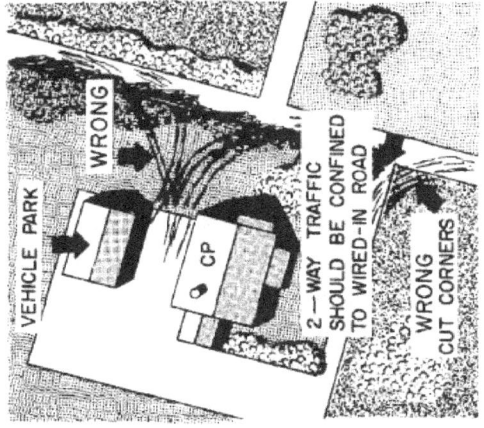

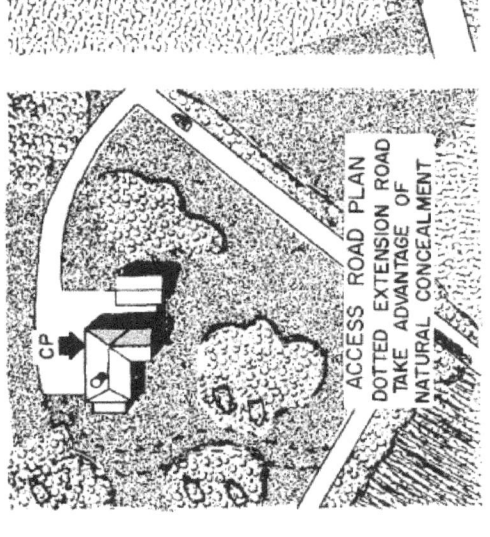

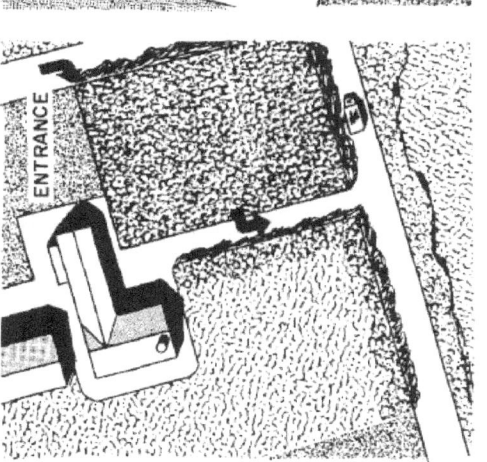

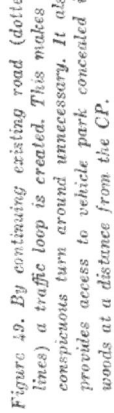

Figure 49. By continuing existing road (dotted lines) a traffic loop is created. This makes a conspicuous turn around unnecessary. It also provides access to vehicle park concealed in woods at a distance from the CP.

Figure 50. Small parking area for visitors. Overhead cover is created by placing natural materials in wire netting. Unless overhead cover is available, visitors must not be permitted to dismount near command post.

Figure 51. Tracks must be controlled and all traffic restricted to existing paths and roads. Edges of road turn-offs, intersections, and short narrow roads subject to heavy military traffic are wired in to prevent conspicuous road widening and corner cutting.

160

Also, when using natural material in the immediate area, go at least 50 yards away from the position you are camouflaging, in order to collect vegetation, dirt, etc. Otherwise, the area around your hide will appear disturbed.

Hopefully this chapter has provided some basic, but crucial information on not being noticed in the contemporary environment (i.e., drones). One would find it odd that at the height of the Vietnam War, the US Army's field manual on camouflage would focus on countering aerial imagery. However, it is shockingly relevant now. One of the phrases of modern warfare is "If you can be seen, you can be killed." Regardless of how many inexperienced Mall Ninjas or Zombie Apocalypse types are out there (and God knows how the attention span and situational awareness of people within our own culture has dropped like a rock over the years), as survivalists, we cannot lower our own operating standards for a second. As mentioned elsewhere in this book, there *will* be rogue elements of professionals out there (Think of Ravenwood Security from the CBS TV series *Jericho*). One designated person (hopefully a subject-matter expert) in your family, retreat group, collective, etc. should be your camouflage coordinator, with everyone else encouraged to provide input (as with all other areas of expertise).

The focus of this chapter is to get people to NOT rely on body armor. In reality, many survivalists do not own any. Therefore, we need to train, and train-to-fight "old school," as has been taught to US Army Infantrymen since at least The Vietnam War. This means primarily one thing: Operating with your rifle from the "prone" position, meaning your body staying flat to the ground.

However, the most important reason for not relying on body armor is because as survivalists, we don't have the same access to medical support that a soldier does. Although there is good, affordable body armor out there that will even stop 5.56 NATO M855 steel penetrator ammo at close range, we still cannot afford to be hit in any extremity, period. Sure, from video footage from Iraq and Afghanistan, you'll see U.S. troops standing around, kneeling, needlessly exposing their bodies to direct fire, etc. In addition to their body armor, they all had a sense of secur ty, knowing that they had immediate access to the best trauma care in the world. However, as survivalists in a collapsed environment, we are already aware of the fact that something as small as an infected cut in our skin can kill us. And, we won't have that same access to medical care. Are you still willing to expose yourself to weapons fire? In addition, are you really willing to take casualties, if those people being shot at are your sons, daughters, husbands, wives, etc? I didn't think so. None of us can afford to be shot in this described environment, period.

This is not meant to discourage people from using their body armor. If your fitness level and patrolling requirements allow (i.e., a quick 15-20 minute circular walk around the perimeter of your retreat), then feel free, as long as it does not otherwise slow you down. Body armor should also be readily handy within your defensive perimeter, in the event of attack, and should also be worn when in a vehicle.

Tactical training schools like Front Sight and Thunder Ranch are great, in teaching basic techniques, holstering and drawing weapons, moving with a rifle, etc. However, a lot of their training focuses on firing while walking, running, both towards a threat, and away from a threat. Laying down your own suppressive fire is a good thing, *if* you are caught alone. However, we need to focus on traditional infantry skills. In combat, the old adage applies: If you can be seen, you can be killed.

In addition, survivalists need to be more concerned with fighting in the defense, and in group tactics such as avoiding contact, and breaking contact (getting away from someone who is shooting at you). This is not to say that post-collapse offensive operations will not be conducted to eliminate a threat, i.e., conducting spoiling attacks on a larger threat-force, liberating an area (See Jim Rawles' *Patriots*), etc.

While this classic Marine-style sitting position might look cool, it is tactically the wrong way to use this type of solid cover.

This is the correct way to use cover. We want to stay in the prone (on our stomachs) whenever possible, and shoot AROUND good ballistic cover, not silhouetting ourselves over the top of it (All of you Mall Ninjas out there in the fancy, overpriced 5.11 tactical clothing are just going to have to deal).

In the urban environment, we also want to be ambidextrous with our weapons. In this photo, our post-collapse survivor is firing left handed.

For movement while under fire, we want to follow the "I'm up, I'm seen, I'm down," three-second rush rule. This rule, ingrained in every modern infantryman since at least the Vietnam War, makes it extremely difficult for anyone with a weapon to draw a bead on you, because by the time that they put you into their weapon sight (even the quick, modern holographic ones), you're already flat on the ground, behind cover and/or concealment, once again. If possible, make sure that where you begin/finish each rush is solid cover: buildings, trees, etc. (the US Army usually refers to a three-to-five second rush, based on the availability of cover).

Also, if you are in direct contact with someone shooting at you (or simply in a dangerous environment), combine this with a complete "combat roll" of your body. Remain behind cover as much as possible while performing your roll (for example, if you are aiming around a tree right-handed, roll to the left) before getting up to start the next rush. Otherwise, you might end-up standing directly into a person's rifle sights.

In this example, this person starts from where everyone should ideally be when halted during movement: Flat on the ground, in the prone position (and ideally behind cover, except in this example).

He starts with a quick, complete combat roll to his left.

Then...

"I'm up..."

"I'm seen..."

"I'm down". To help break your three-second sprint, "bunny hop" on one foot, bend at the knees, then use your buttstock to break the rest of your fall. For all of you AR-types out there, I strongly recommend going back to the original, gov't issue style stocks on your rifles (Besides, it's nice having the extra storage space within the stock).

...And back in a good prone position.

Also, in order to perform these individual techniques, it helps to have a standard, solid stock on your battle rifle. Telescoping, adjustable stocks have their place, but not when you are using your buttstock to break your fall as you end your three-second rushes. Or, in the event of hand-to-hand combat, for that matter. They will eventually become damaged, taking your rifle's buffer assembly with it (in the case of an AR15/M4), making it unserviceable (Besides, as long as your tactics and techniques remain better than your adversaries, you'll eventually acquire your own collection of other people's fancy tactical gear).

The following are examples of buddy-team movement in an urban environment:

A two-man team, aiming right-and-left-handed around cover

While traveling or patrolling in an urban environment, maintain a distance, as in a rural setting, while watching pre-designated sectors. In the above example, the person in the foreground is watching the sides and rear of their traveling direction, while the person in the background is watching the sides and front.

When halting movement, get back into the prone and behind cover, while maintaining your spread. Remember, as survivalists in a collapsed environment, we cannot depend on body armor, immediate trauma care, etc.

"Cover me, I'm moving out." An example of a two-man bounding overwatch. This is how you should move when under fire, or in a dangerous environment. Also, try to remain behind cover as you perform your combat rolls, before getting up to rush to the next position. Watch those rifle muzzles, as you perform your roll. Try not to bump your rifle into brick walls, cement pillars (as in the above photo) etc.

"In position, go!" Once these movements are trained and ingrained in your team members, vocalizations shouldn't be necessary. If under fire for instance, your buddy's weapons fire will be your signal to "go."

If time allows while in a dangerous environment, travel along concealment. Traveling *inside* of concealment is better, except in this case (a row of needled Barberry). Be prepared to high-crawl long distances, if necessary.

These are the techniques that were not only taught to me as

a young infantryman in the early 1980's, but reinforced by the Vietnam Vet instructors that I was blessed to have been trained-by at the US Army's Jungle Warfare School in Panama, in 1983. They are based on decades of historical analysis. While younger generations who have been in Iraq and Afghanistan may scoff at some of this old school training, they need to understand that as survivalists, we cannot afford to be hit in a firefight, period.

Modern US Army infantry training is based on the assumption that despite the limited mobility of extensive body armor, each soldier is supported by the most advanced medical support in history. Yes, I've seen the training drills of modern US Infantrymen, where they remain standing, swiveling their bodies around, while wearing around 70 pounds of reinforced body armor, ammunition, etc.

If patrolling in a wooded area for instance, with ample solid cover against projectiles, we do not need to be weighted down with body armor. In that case, we need to be light, and react quickly. Also, physical fitness will probably be an issue with some of your group members. There are many people out there calling themselves survivalists, who, if you ask them to put on all of their gear, cannot make it more than ten feet outside of their homes.

I do not see a military-style conflict happening within the US any time soon (not to say that American Civil War II *can't* happen), but there are other things to consider here. As we head down the bumpy road of societal decline, there will be more people going postal in public places, shootouts between groups of people, etc. Therefore, we should start visualizing this stuff now, in order to know how to react when we find ourselves in these situations.

In conclusion, as with instructional books in the martial arts, not everyone can learn from a book. Therefore, try to pair-up with a buddy or buddies, in order to practice the techniques described in this chapter. Training with a buddy (or a family member, which is more fun) is the best way to understand what is being conveyed from a book.

While I was finishing-up the previous edition of this book, the summer, 2012 theater shooting in Aurora, Colorado had just taken place. Many of the injuries occurred when people trampled each other while exiting the theater. The smart move, which many experts have stated, is to try to stay put, hit the ground, and try to crawl under something, *depending on the situation*. Also, needless to say, anyone else in the theater with a concealed handgun, carried legally or not, could have saved numerous lives, just by simply returning fire, and at least drawing the fire of this armed coward.

Bugging-out is basically synonymous with evacuating your home, except that you are heading to a pre-arranged retreat location of your own, or someone else's (Hopefully). Bugging out can also be defined by the people who are currently (and strategically) selling their urban and suburban properties, and buying houses and land in rural areas, as far away as possible from urban population centers.

The original use of the term "bugging-out" was from the US Army, which referred to an unplanned retreat or withdrawal. This phrase practically dominated the Korean War, after the Chinese invaded North Korea. The US Army (thanks largely to MacArthur's bumbling, *even after* he had been warned by the CIA) assumed that the Chinese were not going to invade, and were completely unprepared for it, creating one of the most embarrassing moments for the US Army, in military history.[7]

The concept of bugging-out for civilians began with the survivalism expert and author Mel Tappan, in the 1970's, where he assumed that urban population centers would simply lose it, in complete chaos and rampage. Back then, that may have been true, considering the race riots that occurred during the 1960's, the famous New York City blackout of 1977, etc. However, that same demographic majority of Baby Boomers are now in their 60's, and in many cases are overweight, out-of-shape and on multiple prescription drugs (not to say that people in their 60's can't be dangerous).

The bugging-out concept is not for everyone. It depends on your personal wealth, your family and socio-economic situation. It

---

[7]   The US Marine Corps, on the other hand, turned their retreat from the Chosin Reservoir to the North Korean east coast into an intelligently-planned fighting withdrawal, that is regarded as one of the finest moments in Marine Corps history.

also depends on what you think may happen, in a likely scenario. Because of this, the idea of bugging out has some flaws. To begin with, many people jumping on the survivalism band wagon are blindly following what they read or watch, putting together "72-hour bugout kits", planning to evacuate their home. If you ask many of these survivalism newbies if they have a bugout location, many of them begin to hesitate and mumble. In other words, they don't have a bugout plan, and realistically, may not need one at this time, since they are not thinking this stuff through, to begin with.

One trend that is picking-up speed as we continue through long-term societal decline is suicide. Data collected from the U.S. National Center for Health Statistics indicates that since 2010, suicide within the U.S. has actually surpassed traffic fatalities. This growing trend is an important factor, when formulating any decision to bug-out of your traditional community. What would be the point of bugging-out, if half of all of your neighbors have already killed themselves (of course, in a long-term scenario, we still need to visualize what may come after this wave of suicide, if the rate of collapse decides to speed up)?

Cormac McCarthy seemed to understand this when he wrote his fictional masterpiece, *The Road*. McCarthy intentionally makes it unclear what the actual apocalyptic event was (based on an interview he gave, along with some other clues, I believe it was a nuclear strike. Either way, a "nuclear winter" effect was created). In a flashback scene several years after the event (as in the movie), the wife discusses the pointlessness of continuing to live, as there seemed to be no outside help whatsoever, they had a child, born after the event, and besides, "most of their neighbors had already done it" (paraphrase). In addition, the wife was concerned about their chances of surviving any large, heavily armed groups, anyway, and what they would do to her.

As a reminder folks, this is *not* what survivalism is about: It's about not giving up, not quitting.

We should also take a look at the European countries currently undergoing austerity measures: Greece and Spain, in particular, where suicides *really* began skyrocketing, as of 2008. Greece is also in the process of denuding its forests, in search of firewood to keep warm with, during Winter.[8] The people in these countries are currently experimenting with hundreds of alternative economies, to include communal living, cashless communities, local currencies, etc. However, there has been no "bugging-out," in any of these countries, in the survivalist sense (other than family members and friends "doubling up," in addition to the fact that many people in these countries probably cannot afford to relocate out of cities, if they wanted to).

Hurricane Katrina and its aftermath was a different story, however. This was a classic, Mel Tappan I-told-you-so moment. Due to the socio-economic conditions in New Orleans such as poverty, racial intolerance, and police corruption, this helped create the perfect storm, literally. Add to this the ineptitude on the part of the federal government's response (also driven by racial and political intolerance, all the way from the White House on-down), and you got an outright societal collapse moment that not only vindicated the preparedness / survivalism movement, but actually propelled it to a newer level of popularity.

In this case, the smart (and financially capable) people did bug out ahead of the storm. Hopefully, they were able to evacuate with *all* of their valuable tangibles, in addition to important records, family keepsakes, etc.

In the case of the people who stayed, such as the economically disadvantaged and infirm, downtown New Orleans turned into a living hell, creating misery on a large scale, not recently seen in American history. These people in downtown

---

[8] Dr. Nate Hagens of the Post Carbon Institute, a well-known authority on global resource depletion, is currently (as of this writing) researching the depletion of Greece's forests, and the potential effects. The stripping of forests for fuel is an area of concern for Peak Oil collapse theorists, in particular.

New Orleans were stranded for five days without any supply of food and water. Looting was rampant throughout the area, with members of local law enforcement also taking part. Other police were pinned-down in their own police stations by sniper fire.

The people who were able to evacuate have had their own stories to tell, and through websites such as SurvivalBlog.com, have provided invaluable information for the rest of us, based on what they did / should have done better.

The following is from the Survivalblog archives, from September 13, 2006. It almost reads like something from a post-collapse novel:

What Happens After: Observations on Hurricane Katrina

Just a few notes about my experiences with Hurricane Katrina a year later. On the evening that Katrina passed our retreat, my partner and I began to make our way back to our homes (less than 30 miles) and businesses to secure them – (both firearms related). We chose to take different routes, him on foot, and me in my truck with my dogs & supplies. The routes required pushing and/or cutting trees, poles, fences and all manner of lines and debris from the road ways. The few roads that could be made passable with chain saws and simple tools tended to concentrate people and vehicles. While resting between swinging a chain saw (several folks were taking turns) one of my dogs (the cur) became highly agitated. Knowing her reputation for correctly gauging people I got a good grip on my (Model) 1911. As my truck window was already down (heat and humidity were horrible) I watched a character approach – he was intently looking into each vehicle he passed. Once he reached my truck he approached the driver's side and wanted to buy gas that I was carrying (having it in the open was a mistake). I explained that it was not for sale – I would need it when I got home. Then he became very belligerent and indicated that he was going to take it to get to New Orleans. It became clear that the situation was critical, so with well practiced motion I introduced him to the 1911, at which point he wisely elected to be somewhere else. I realized that safety was off and I had taken up slack on the trigger – I had committed to use deadly force in a split second, right or wrong. The event did diffuse the situation immediately and efficiently. It took 12 + hours to traverse less than 30 miles in the truck. My partner made the trip by hiking and catching a ride in less than 4 hours.

Over the period of the next few days the world took on a totally different aspect. We were under martial law – no firearms, ammunition, or alcohol and a sunset to sunrise curfew. As both our businesses were firearms related there was the need for a degree of security around the clock. The local law enforcement was stretched so thin as to be of no response value. As we are just north of the Mississippi/Louisiana border, the community grew from 12,000 to around 51,000 in a few days. Having prepared (largely in part to your novel "Patriots") we were able to meet those whom chose not to observe the curfew, and probe the "edges", in a decisive manner. Generators helped light one of the businesses, but they are very noisy, so we had to depend on the dogs. In the other we chose to be completely dark, and depend on the dogs for early warning.

We learned that a schedule for sleep, chores, eating, and duty helped offset the elevated "wired" condition. In the planning I chose a home with a "artesian" free flowing well (~ 3-5 psi) , however without power for wells many folks uncapped free flowing wells in the area stopping the flow due to the relieved pressure points. Some municipal water was available on a limited basis. Water quality was a concern. With temperatures in the mid to high nineties and humidity there as well water for animals and electrolytes for people were hugely importantly (those containing sugar were not as effective, and seemed to be harmful).

We came through fine, and the lessons learned have been incorporated. Electricity took 17 days to [be restored to] my home and phone service [restoration] 10 weeks. No local government help was in evidence for five days. Almost all of the supplies and relief in the first few days came through the local churches (they were and still are the most effective distribution system). During events like these dealing with otherwise good people has severely changed our approach to people and denial. Some where near 80% of the people in the area are still not making any preparations against significant events. The mental toll it has taken on the community is still visible today.

Lessons Learned:
1. Carry what you need but keep as much out of

sight as possible
2. Expect to have to dissuade those whom feel entitled to your supplies
3. The aspect of deadly force is an effective deterrent – be prepared to use it or abandon your provisions
4. Know and pay attention to your early warning systems – animal or electronic
5. Big dogs and alert dogs are a great help
6. Practice, shoot, practice, plan, practice

The bottom line is that in any event, there are unforeseen consequences. The time that you set down with your group and define what, when, and where will be of paramount value. Understand that some of the group may not make it (some of ours was trapped far away) the rest can and will have the resources available, and take up the slack, until such a time that all can join up. I do laugh easier, shoot more and plan more effectively now. Remember: technology may help but your brain will save your life! - DGS

Bugging-in is the exact opposite, due to limited resources, family, or, most importantly, the realization that bugging out is not logical. Where would you go? How do you bring all of your larder with you? Or more importantly, why would you leave your home, period, during a chaotic societal breakdown, if you simply did not need to? Especially if your security, food storage, and self sustaining means of food and water are in place?

Even in suburbia, you may already be well-set, with plenty of land around your house to grow food, security measures, and military and/or law enforcement experience in securing a perimeter. Your home may be adjacent to a creek, or you may have had the insight to drop a well into your backyard (city-permitted, or not), or maybe even a rain-catchment cistern system. Why would you want to leave all this, for somewhere else more questionable, unless it was an all-ready, well established retreat?

The website *Survival Acres: Sustainable Living and Common Sense* (http://survivalacres.com/wordpress/) put out an article on April 18, 2012 that was highly critical of the bugging out concept, called *The Fallacy of Bugging Out*. It is a rather long quoted piece, but contains very valuable and realistic insights:

> Many websites, blogs and forums have covered the topic of bugging out in excruciating detail, all under the assumption that this will be a necessary escape plan for many of us when the proverbial shit hits the fan. This notion is predicated upon the belief that escape and evasion, necessary for your immediate survival will be a (likely) event that you must plan and prepare for now.
>
> However, nothing could be further from the real and actual truth. This cherished myth is a deceptive and dangerous notion that has little place in reality. I've long held a stance *against* this notion because in nearly all cases and all situations, this is a very bad idea with oftentimes fatal consequences. Bugging out is *embracing* the refugee lifestyle - a very bad idea. Refugees throughout history have fared very badly, suffered extreme hardship and deprivation, with many not surviving the experience. There is a far better alternative to this.
>
> The rejection of the "bug out" mythology flies in the face of the so-called 'expert advice' and theory being proposed by many websites and authors,

who are also very active in selling products and gear specifically oriented around this concept. You could say quite rightly, that there is indeed a agenda at work here, but it is not one in your best interests. Hold onto your pockets and read on.

Bugging out entails leaving everything you **are**, and everything you **own**, and everything you *use*, *day in and day out*, and everything you cannot **carry** or **transport** with you, behind. Not only behind, but *inaccessible, unusable and abandoned.* Potentially forever...

...How long could you hold out? Not long. The reasons are many, but they are sound.

The *need* to bug out is an exceedingly tiny reality — a future event that will probably never happen. But it is not a *zero* possibility (nothing is, not even an alien invasion). Yet this topic still receives a ridiculous amount of attention despite its extremely low probability, which makes no sense at all. The reason is because *escapism* is thought to be a 'solution' versus contributing to the problem. It's not, as the points above demonstrate.

Running — from whatever the problem is, usually ensures that you are taking your problems *with* you. Only if your life is in *immediate* danger does running offer a better opportunity then staying put and dealing with the problem. Running does not make problems go away, it will very often make them much worse...

To The Woods

Bugging out is usually assumed to mean "to the woods" where survivors, patriots, militia, end-timers and others will be making "their last stand" (apparently together, whether they like it or not) while roasting hotdogs and marshmallows. Instead, it will be the last man standing over a pile of rotted and half-eaten *corpses*, since the food and supplies and the notions of 'living off the land' will have died out with the last slaughtered deer to be found...

...Campsites, caves and hidey-holes will have become armed, dirty and infested encampments of hungry and desperate men (the surviving women would have long since been forced into prostitution and slavery), all fighting over the remaining scraps to be found (and newcomers showing up) necessary for their survival. Informants, traitors, thieves, murderers, rapists and thugs will quickly become the defining characteristic, with the strongest ruling (or eating) the weak. Those who arrive "first" will potentially be better prepared to prey upon the late-comers or the weak, so if you are still planning on trying this, get your seat at the table *early*.

Think not? This is exactly what happens during civil wars and internal conflicts when a country turns against itself. The war in Bosnia saw tens of thousands of murders, rapes and thefts as the people turned on each other. It was a fight for survival, for food, for weapons, for money, for women.

It has happened all over the world, and it will happen again. Whenever there is not enough to go around, and whenever there is strife, secrecy and conflict, those involved will resort to whatever methods of survival that they have to in order that they might live another day by whatever means possible. It will be no picnic, no romantic "retreat into the woods" where faith, truth, righteousness or rebellion will flourish and grow. Instead, it will be a bloodbath where the young, old and the weak succumb the quickest. I suggest you bring lots of Tabasco sauce, as it does make the meat taste better.

...Inversely, you could also expect smart and prepared communities to expel, exterminate and hunt down these refugees if things get way out of hand, exacerbating an already bad situation. Forget for a moment the military or law enforcement going after these woodland refugees (a topic unto itself), the locals themselves will not be the helping hand that you may have naively come to expect, especially if you or your gang have already trod upon their welcome mat. They're trying to survive too, and live normal, unfettered lives as best they can. They don't need nor appreciate you coming along and messing things up. Camping out in their back yard or nearby forests will often pit you against them in violent and lethal ways. And they will be far more adept then you are, outlasting you because they will have the infrastructure and support network to do so.

Survivalism is only rarely about 'surviving in the woods'. Rather, survivalism is about *living*, and staying alive, and how you might do that while experiencing as few hardships as you can (Author's Emphasis). Bugging out to the woods to survive your end-time fantasies is going to be a quick path to death for the majority of people that try this route. There is a better alternative to this.

Staying Alive

Bugging out is never quite what everyone seems to think it is, where living off the land and finding adequate nutrition and staying healthy is grossly overlooked. Many people claim that they can "do it", yet return year after year from hunting season empty handed. When the beer runs out, they head home. Or when the food is bland or gone, they're beating tracks as fast as they can to the nearest restaurant. These 'survivalists' and 'outdoorsman' will not survive their voluntary refugee status by bugging out, but they will (if they show up, far from home) be a serious problem for the locals.

You will burn up a tremendous amount of calories (as much as 3 - 4 times as normal) while trying to live off the land. Finding and building shelter, hunting and gathering for food and water, providing heat, establishing security and working and waking / walking for long hours at a time, will cause you to expend far more calories then you will be taking in. Even if you are very well supplied, you won't be for long (you cannot carry enough). Foraging for food will very rarely provide enough calories versus what you are expending while looking. You will quickly go into a calorie deficit, burning off fats and muscles as your body adapts to your new environment and demands.

I've seen lot of ill-informed discussion of 'nomadic lifestyle' whereas the individual or group is roaming about, living off the land. This notion is pure B.S., as it is calorie-deficient, ill-advised for security reasons and will increase the risk of injury and health issues. You will need to *preserve* calories — not expend them (if you can).

Calorie deficiency cannot last very long (mere days in most cases) before your health diminishes and your strength drops. You risk hypothermia, vitamin deficiencies and a higher risk of contracting illness and injury due to your weakened condition. Unless your nutritional needs are met and you are able to also stay warm and dry, avoiding hypothermia (core temperature drop) and frostbite / exposure, then it is just a matter of time before you become incapacitated, unable to effectively help yourself.

There are countless examples of 'modern day survivalists' who have found this out, believing that they too could live off the land and survive, but lacking the skills and experience to do so. Additionally, our forests are not the cornucopia of food waiting to be plucked many seem to think, they're vastly depleted monocultures of trees, lacking sufficient edible foods and wildlife. Some of these people wound up dead, others were found or rescued. All of them learned that foraging for sufficient nutrition and calories is why we have modern farms — it is the most efficient way of meeting our nutritional needs. Even growing your own food at home in a controlled environment (garden) with a plentiful supply of soils, seeds, water, tools and time is extremely difficult, if not nearly impossible for most of us (really) to meet all your daily nutritional needs, all while leading a far less demanding lifestyle then living off in the woods in survival mode. I've long been advocating sustainable living and raising your own food, but here in the woods where I live, I cannot even grow half of the food I need to stay alive and healthy, let alone expect to hunt it down. Nor can I grow enough to feed my family, compounding the nutritional needs required...

...Ultimately, this then is the far better solution — **bugging in**, back to safety, food, heat, clothing, medical attention and survival. If you truly think that you foresee a need to bug out — then revise your plans to bug in to a new location within civilization where you can find (or work for) food, clothing, shelter, safety and security (including an income) where your survival is a far more sure thing. This is the only long-term answer there really is. You will also be in a much better situation to deal with whatever the problem was in the first place that caused you to leave.

I do not have a bug out bag anymore, since it no longer makes any sense to me to have one. I do have cash, toys, tools, vehicles and other things of interest at my disposal. Disappearing off into the woods is a dead end and it will not work for the vast majority of people that would try this. You would have to come out sooner then you think (if you survive) and return to life within civilization somewhere. You're not going to live off the land indefinitely, and not even as long as you may think, so it makes far more sense in your 'escape plan' to prepare for living someplace else instead.

The entire concept of bugging out truly needs to be **redefined** to fit within the parameters of reality and how this would really work for the vast majority of people. *Leaving* for reasons of safety, security, natural disasters or some other valid reason is perfectly acceptable — but where you go and how you will plan on surviving while you are there seems to be where this theory falls flat on its face against reality. Having the means to leave, but having some place to go, where you can find safety, food, shelter and **sustainability** is key to a true "bug out" plan. Planning on disappearing into the woods is in all probability one of the worst ideas you could attempt. You would have to come out sooner or later, weakened, possibly sick or injured, broke, destitute and impoverished — a true self-made refugee. Basically, a dumb idea all around; one that should only be tried in the most extreme circumstances and only for the adept.

I believe that this article's logic is inescapable, regarding the bugging out concept. As the author concludes, only consider bugging out as a long term plan, in the current societal context.

Again, as survivalists, we plan for the absolute worse-case scenario. There are reasons to evacuate your home, depending on the region of the country you live in.

In the event of large-scale fire, for instance, if you live in a rural or suburban area that is prone to them, then the traditional bugout plan, with grab & go backpack applies. A forest fire can move so quickly, that many have been consumed by firestorms as they ran back into their homes for last-minute items.

However, for a sudden ecological or societal event, bugging in can be a very smart decision. Just as in people being trampled in a panic as they run from a crazed gunman, a sudden, mass exodus from the suburbs to the country can create its own self-fulfilling prophecy, as had occurred during the evacuations ahead of

Hurricane Rita (the largest single evacuation in U.S. History). In Texas alone, the combination of severe gridlock and excessive heat led to between 90 and 118 deaths even before the storm itself arrived. For instance, Interstate 10 became a giant linear parking lot for hundreds of miles, where vehicles ran out of fuel, people were stranded without food or water, and elderly people got killed as their oxygen cylinders exploded.

However, you will have to be prepared for the bugging –in scenario, which means that at this time, you will be going tactical. In a neighborhood where less than half of the people are remaining (hypothetically), there will most likely be no neighborhood organizing. In addition, your true predators will appear: People who clearly do not belong in the neighborhood, and believe that they are tougher than the situation itself (and probably are). These looters initially will look for homes that have been vacated, and will be out primarily at night. There are basically two ways to deal with this, in order to get undesirables to leave the neighborhood.

In the absence of the rule of law, and you notice some backwards-hat wearing, tattooed, earrings in weird places-type individuals, you could simply shoot these people on-sight. That is usually an attention-getter, if you do not mind leaving a few decomposing bodies lying around.

In a more realistic short-term, or relatively short term regional disaster (Hurricane Katrina, for instance), you could use silent weapons, such as slingshots, pellet guns, etc. to injure these people. If you take an eye out, oh well. In reality, criminals, being vulnerable themselves, do not go to the police to tell them "Gee officer, I was in a neighborhood I have no business in, looking for a place to steal from, and someone hit me in the eye with a pellet gun..."

If people have left your neighborhood due to an economic shock, such as a collapse of the dollar, where the trucks are no longer backing-up to the local Wal-Mart, then the remaining people, one-to-two months into a long term or indefinite disaster will probably be coming to your house, hoping to borrow food, or toiletry items. Just let them know that you don't have any yourself, or make-up some other story. In this situation, even appearing ill can go a long way in making people believe you have nothing of value (as mentioned in the previous chapter on dealing with refugees).

Hopefully, in this scenario you are not already known as the neighborhood survivalist. In a situation where your neighbors are not aware of your preps a couple of months into a crisis, they may be less patient, if they see that you are well-fed, and clean. Hopefully you have not been going outside during the day, and have been performing all of your outside duties at night, in a tactical mode. In this scenario, as the author "Joe Nobody" has mentioned in his writings, **do not open the door for anyone, period**. You can tell them "whatever" from the other side of a locked door, with a loaded weapon.

So folks, I think you get the idea. While there is a time and circumstance to evacuate your home, for any other type of societal event, we should probably stay at home, where we have all of our resources, such as our stored larder, our food-producing gardens, etc. If you are financially independent, self-employed, retired, etc, then relocating in the present to a lighter populated region (such as Jim Rawles' "American Redoubt" in the continental northwest region of the US) is probably a good idea.

However, as of my own research, to include my interviewing of rural land owners in particular, in the present, there is a certain trend toward the targeting of rural properties by burglars. In these areas there are no neighbors (even the ones you do not know that well) to have any eyes on your home. In the current operating environment (slow collapse, depending on the region you currently reside in), bugging-in *within* suburbia is **very likely the best current solution**.

Remember: The ideal form of survivalism is to avoid societal (or personal) upheaval in the first place. Many people have created their own worst self-fulfilling prophecies by either moving to homes in rural areas within the US, or expatriating themselves to places like Mexico, where they end-up living in an environment of much more crime, corruption, etc. Again, assess your own situation regarding possible scenarios, neighbors, sustainability, defendability, etc.

XVIII Bartering and Haggling

"If I had my life to live over again, I would elect to be a trader of goods rather than a student of science. I think barter is a noble thing.

—Albert Einstein

The ability to barter and profitably trade will become very important in the event that money becomes hyper-inflated, or is in short supply (deflation). In the case of societal disaster or because you want to live simply and as far from the monetized economy as possible, bartering will be your primary means of obtaining products and services you and your family need.

When you barter, you exchange a surplus item or skill for another item or service that you need. The exchange occurs without money changing hands. Determine what items you have to barter with, whether they are physical items, or skills and services. Assign a monetary value to these items, skills, and services (has anyone reading this ever played *Fallout*, the post-apocalyptic, late1990's computer role playing game? Highly recommended, particularly Fallout II and III). Then decide what it is that you need and assign a monetary value to it. This is the basis of your exchange.

It's a good idea to keep survival barter items on hand that other people will find desirable to barter for. For example, specialty foods like butter and homemade jellies, handmade items like a knit scarf or sweater can be very desirable. Even candy and chocolates can make good items to barter. Do you have duplicates of some items around the house? Maybe you have two sets of silverware, extra toys, or games. These extras easily lend themselves to bartering. When the Soviet Union collapsed, the streets of Moscow were one giant flea market, where people desperately attempted to sell their children's toys, extra pairs of shoes, etc.

Alcohol and tobacco are some of the best barter items during a period of societal collapse, due to their high potential value. In Europe, during and immediately after WW II (and during the more recent Bosnian Civil War) this was definitely the case. It's true that these items will be in short supply if trucks no longer deliver these items to our local stores.

Common brands of liquor, such as Whiskey, Tequila, Vodka, etc. can be placed in ammo cans with other packaging material, to keep them protected. And, as mentioned earlier in my reference to the inflation preparedness book *The Alpha Strategy*, can make great value per cubic foot of storage.

If storing cigarettes, make sure they are common brands, non-menthol, and to store them in a vacuum sealed state, if possible. Conducting my own research, I have learned that someone in need of a cigarette will not worry too much about the lack of freshness. However, menthols, if stored improperly, can actually spoil a cigarette, even for a heavily addicted smoker.

An ideal way of storing cigarettes would be to stack the individual packs inside of an ammo can, with one, or a couple of oxygen absorbers thrown in. A "Fat-50" can (larger than a standard .50 cal. can) or 20mm ammo can would probably be an ideal size. Just one of these, loaded with packs of various brands of non-menthol cigarettes and a couple of quickly and carefully handled oxygen absorbers could make someone fairly wealthy, on the other side of collapse, either short-term, or indefinite. In addition, the beauty of using ammo cans is that they will eventually vacuum-seal on their own, even without the use of oxygen absorbers, due to temperature change. This is why you may eventually hear some of them "burp," from time-to-time.

A good use of a "tipping point" news story ("we just attacked

Iran," etc.), would be to "zig," while everyone else "zags." In other words, while everyone else rushes the nearest Wal Mart for groceries, you go to a stand-alone cigarette shop, and buy a few cartons of popular brands. Or, if you are military, a military reservist, retired military, or live on an Indian Reservation, you buy tax-free from those locations. Since you should have your beans, bullets and band aids already squared away (and want to avoid violent crowds, etc.), you can use the last hours, or minutes to buy barterables. You never know what you might have left-out in your preps, after the situation starts. This is the primary reason we are concerned with post-collapse bartering.

In a worst-case societal scenario, precious metals, pre-1965 US coinage, etc., may be regarded as worthless, due to their lack of tangible functionality (you can't shoot it, wear it, or eat it). As in the 1990's Bosnian conflict, full-cartridge ammunition (and possibly some reloading components, like primers, bullets, spent brass, reloading dies, etc.) will probably serve as currency. Even at the time of this writing, many survivalists and preppers are no longer interested in buying physical gold or silver.

Do you have skills that other people would find valuable enough to trade their goods and services to get? Some examples of skills to barter are sewing, knitting, baking, cooking, cleaning, teaching, babysitting, gunsmithing, armed security/bodyguard, yard work, gardening, musical ability, carpentry, plumbing, and roofing. As you can see, everyone has some sort of skill to trade. Take an inventory of skills and items you have and begin to use these to trade for what you want. Trading your skills should actually be your priority, as compared to trading any tangible items.

Jim Rawles at Survivalblog once posted a self-written article in October of 2008, which to this day is the best piece I have ever seen on the subject of bartering and haggling. It is written from both the attendee, and the vendor perspectives, of events such as swap meets, flea markets, horse trading events and gun shows:

The Savvy Barterer--References, Skills, and Tools for TEOTWAWKI Barter

One of my long-standing Precepts is that every prepared individual should be ready for both barter and dispensing charity. Today, I'll be briefly discussing barter. Being ready to barter is **not** just a matter of having **a pile of "stuff"** to barter. While barter and charity logistics are important, what is even more important is what is between your ears.

A Bazaar Experience

Bartering takes practice. Dickering is an acquired skill. Short of buying yourself a plane ticket to Marrakech, I suggest that you start attending gun shows, garage sales, and flea markets. Learn how to haggle.

One of my long standing Rawlesian Precepts is having the skills and material acquired to conduct barter in a post-collapse society. Much has been written about what goods to keep on hand for bartering. But precious little has been discussed in survivalist literature on the *skills* required to barter effectively, and how to protect yourself from fraud.

I recommend that you practice bartering on a very small scale at first, to sharpen your eye for value and your ability to dicker in a manner that will resu t in a fair trade. (Mutually agreeable and mutually beneficial.) The occasional transaction where you end up slighted is hardly cause for concern. But unless you develop the proper bartering skills, you'll end up on the weaker side of bargains again and again, and thus fritter away your tangible working capital. The attributes that will put you in a superior bartering position include specific knowledge about what is being traded, knowledge about who's sitting on the other side of the table, and good old-fashioned "horse trading sense".

Knowledge and References

The more you know about the goods being exchanged the better you'll be able to dicker. Armed with this knowledge, you'll be able to honestly, yet persuasively talk up the virtues of your own goods, while politely talking down the defects of your trading partner's goods. Hence, the greater your technical knowledge of the goods, the better. Take the time to study and develop an 'appraiser's eye' for the condition of used merchandise, the relative value of goods from one maker versus another, and knowledge of the overall market. With that knowledge you can articulate the scarcity of any particular item in your barter stock. (After all, as with any other free market transaction, the key factor in determining value is the supply-demand ratio.) If you are trading for a collectible item then knowing how scarce they are can put you at a tremendous advantage in negotiation. It is important to **gather as many references as possible** about the items that you plan to barter. Francis Bacon said it best: "Knowledge is power." You need to authoritatively know which maker, model, variation, grade, year of production, etc. to look for. Product expertise helps makes you a savvy buyer or seller. There are dozens of references on specific types of tool, guns, and collectibles that are valuable to keep on hand. For example, two of the most important ones that I 've found for firearms are: "*The Blue Book of Gun Values*" and

"*Flayderman's Guide to Antique Firearms and Their Values.*"

Similarly, knowing exactly how to properly gauge the condition of a used item is quite important. For example, with firearms, the percentage of original bluing remaining, cracks or wear to a gun's stock, bore condition, chamber condition, bolt face erosion, action tightness, headspace, and so forth all make a huge difference in the value of a used gun.

Detailed knowledge is also crucial when determining the value of a rare coin. (For most of us, that knowledge is too specialized. It can take many years to develop coin grading skills, so a novice can get in over his head very easily. The difference between an MS-66 coin and an MS-68 coin is very subtle, yet that difference can mean *thousands* of dollars difference in a coin's price. I therefore recommend that novices only trade professionally graded coins that have been graded and sealed (or "slabbed") by either PCGS or NGC. A coin dealer Blue Sheet is a crucial reference for measuring the current value of coins with particular mint marks and dates, in any given grade on the Sheldon Scale. Even having an out-of-date Blue Sheet is better than nothing, since it will show **relative values** of coins, which change fairly gradually. Again, this is not for a novice, or part-time dabbler. (FWIW, even though I have been buying rare coins for more than 20 years, I still consider myself effectively a "novice" level since I don't get frequent coin grading practice. Hence, I only buy slabs. ("A man has got to know his limitations.")

Tools

To be ready to barter with **bullion** gold coins or scrap gold it is important to have a touchstone, an acid test kit, test needles, a very accurate scale, and a set of **Fisch coin authenticity dimensional gauges (Author's Note: I have a set, and they are awesome, elegantly simple devices to determine coin authenticity).**

When bartering for canned goods it's important to have a Julian Calendar (since some packers use Julian dates) and a hard copy of this chart showing how to decipher date of pack codes from various canners and packers.

For liquid fuel it's important to know if the fuel has been contaminated or adulterated. ..

For batteries, it's important to have a voltmeter...

For examining the fine details of just about anything...a jeweler's loupe (magnifying glass) is a must.

For evaluating firearms, as a minimum buy a 6 foot tape measure and a fiber optic bore inspection light.

Dickering Tactics

Above and beyond getting technical knowledge is the hard to quantify "people skill" of dickering. Dickering skills can take years to develop. Part of this is learning how to "read" the face and body language of the gent on the other side of the table. How anxious is he to unload something that he has, or to acquire something that you have? How quick they are to make or accept an offer is a key indicator. And if there is a savvy trader sizing *you* up, you have to learn to keep a "poker face", not revealing how excited you are to see a particular item being offered.

Take your time in carefully examining any item offered to you. This accomplishes two things. Firstly, it gives you the opportunity to spot any flaws, defects or signs of wear on the item being offered. Secondly, the more time that you spend examining the item will lead the seller to subconsciously start to doubt the value of what he is offering. If you're in a flea market or gun show situation once you have an item in your hands you are essentially free to examine it without fear of someone else buying it. Take your time!

If you make an offer for an item, and it is rejected, or the counter offer made is ridiculously low, then the very best thing you can do is put the item back down on the table. This psychologically distances you from the item, and again, makes the seller begin to doubt it's value. In the dickering process one of the most valuable phrases that you can use is **"Is that the best you can do?"** If the seller won't budge, and you are close to an acceptable price, the next best thing to do is to offer to sweeten the deal with additional goods offered on your side of the bargain. If you still can't reach an agreement it probably wouldn't hurt to subtly talk down the value of what's being offered to you, and talk up the value of what you are offering. "This is a mighty fine *widget* it's too bad about *this crack* and this *wear*... If it weren't for that, I think your asking price would be fair."

The next most valuable thing you can learn to say is to **say nothing**. After making an offer and receiving a counter offer, silently start counting to twenty. There is something about a long pause that causes all but the most stalwart dickerer to want to fill that silence And nine times out of ten, they will fill that silence with another offer, usually one that is more agreeable.

As a last resort, if you are still at an impasse in reaching an mutually-agreeable trade, your tool of last resort is to thank the seller and start to walk away from the table. This will be your final gauge of just how anxious the seller is to move his merchandise. If you hear "Wait, wait, wait, come back here...", then you know that the seller still has room to negotiate on price or quantities. Keep in mind however, that this is **a dangerous tactic**. Once you walk away from a table without he seller voicing objection, but return later, you have subconsciously boxed yourself into the previously-offered price. If you come back later for the same item, the seller will know that you are anxious to purchase it, and did not find a better deal for a comparable item elsewhere, so they'll probably hold to the same price.

When selling, keep in mind that you can negotiate downwards, but not upwards. Always make your initial asking price somewhat higher than what you really want out of it. Some people will not agree to even a good deal, unless they can extract at least one price concession from you. So, set a fairly high price, and then negotiate downward.

If your counterpart brings an item to offer to you,

but that item is of no interest to you, always thank him for his time: 'Thanks, but I'm not interested in that right now. Do you have any X available?", describing what you are looking for in trade. Remember, a sales venue is an opportunity to gather information about other items a seller may have available, but may not physically have with them. It may not hurt to make arrangements to see them at the next event, reminding them to bring those items so you can make a deal next time...

...When approaching a vendors booth or table for the first time it is important to first wait until the vendor has finished dealing with any previous customers. Don't interrupt a man when he's making a deal! Smile and make eye contact, and if appropriate for the venue, introduce yourself and shake hands. If you are a fellow vendor, it's important to wear your badge, or otherwise make it known that you also have a table or booth. This lets the seller know that he is talking to a *wholesale* rather than retail customer. This can make a tremendous difference when negotiating price. Even if the vendor appears to have a pile of worthless junk on his table (with perhaps a few nice items of interest) make a point of expressing your admiration for his merchandise. Say something like "You've got a real nice inventory here" or "I can see that you have good taste in *widgets*". This is an important step in developing rapport with you counterpart. While it doesn't hurt to point out a defect on an individual item while negotiating for it, **do not** "run down" the quality or condition of everything that you see. Doing so could skunk the entire deal-making process. OBTW, don't be shy about pointing out defects in your own merchandise. "Oh, in case didn't noticed, there is one dent here..." That lets your customer know that you are reputable.

Another key aspect of understanding buying and selling psychology is the "stage of the game". At the beginning of a show or sale most journeymen sellers arrive inventory rich, and cash poor. Near the end of the show, they will likely have more cash (or precious metals) on hand and then will be in a better position to make offers. Although some of the best items may have already been sold, one of the best times to make a purchase or trade is near the end of a show, when some sellers have had a "slow show" At flea markets and gun show wait until *just before* the vendor's "tear down" and pack-up time begins. Depending on their situation they might feel desperate to make a good sale or a couple of good swaps so that they can feel that they've made the show worthwhile. So, if you saw an item earlier in the show, and could not negotiate an agreeable price, wait for the end of the sales event. This, BTW, is particularly valuable tactic if the item in question is particularly bulky or heavy. It is the unspoken goal of every seller to "go home *light*".

If you encounter a seller that has the sort of merchandise that you think would be of future interest, then it's important to get that seller's particulars so that you can contact him later. Take copious notes. The same applies when you encounter a seller that has a particularly valuable area of expertise or a rare stock of items--especially spare parts. These are people well worth "networking" with.

...In closing, barter takes time to learn. Invest that time. Also invest in the proper references. Lastly, invest in a stock of top quality barter goods that you predict will be sought-after in a post collapse world. With the right goods and the requisite knowledge, you and your family will never starve.

Again, this is the best beginner's primer that I have ever seen written on the subject of trading tangibles.

However, I do not agree with every piece of advice that Rawles gives. I had omitted portions of this quoted piece, such as "never trading hard for soft," which I think can be confusing to the average person being introduced to this area of preparedness.

Another omitted portion had to do with image. Jim Rawles recommends that people "dress down," particularly if they are operating as a vendor. However, as I have discovered myself as a vendor at various events, attendees really do not care about what you are wearing. The large crowd seems to act as one big dumb brain, with little visual awareness, to begin with. Therefore, they are not going to notice at all what you are wearing. So feel free to wear your $1000.00 MTM Military Ops watches, or your Danner tactical boots.

In the current operating/economic environment, what they are looking for is price comparisons for a given item that they want. The smart people at these events will look at **all** of the tables at a given event, **before** initiating any purchases. In other words, as a vendor, for the first two hours of an event, you may not get very many sales, if at all. Then, suddenly, you may get overwhelmed with paying-customers, about two hours into it, if you are low-balling your competitors by even a dollar (or even 50 cents, in some cases). Currently, what I have discovered at many public events is that you literally have to hit the GDP (Generally Dumb Public) with the visual equivalent of a two-by-four, in order to get them to notice *anything* on your table, anyway (depending on locale. Some crowds are just smarter than others).

The bottom line: Learn the crowd, and learn how the crowd thinks. It really does function as one big (dumb) brain. For further study on this subject, I highly recommend the Adam Curtis BBC documentary *Century of the Self*, about Edward Bernays (Sigmund Freud's rascally little nephew), and the history of public relations. It is an intellectually deep, revealing documentary, and covers a variety of subjects regarding the crowd, in an age of mass democracy. It wouldn't surprise me if this documentary was banned outright within the U.S., from play by PBS, etc (since the 1970's, when have they ever shown documentaries that ask, or reveal anything about our society, anyway?).

In addition, event attendees who always insist on haggling (particularly for high-demand, rare items, such as ammunition) can be outright irritating to vendors. Many vendors already know the availability of an item, and their price targets (a.k.a., *price equilibrium*) for specific items: That is, the highest dollar price that something "moves" at, where supply and demand meet.

Your more veteran vendors will experiment with prices, starting high, then bringing them down, while observing the public's response. For example, if someone is trying to sell used ammo cans at $18.00, virtually no one may buy them, *even if it is cheaper* than what is being sold by other vendors. If, however they drop the price to $17.00 per can, then suddenly everyone starts crowding around their table to buy them. It is simply a weird phenomenon of group behavior. These same vendors are mentally tougher than the crowd, and will refuse to haggle, since they already know the prices at which their stuff moves at.[9]

Although hopefully we'll have all the stuff we'll need when a societal collapse or anything else occurs, there is still a good chance that we left something out. In addition, for those in an

---

[9] In other words, they are immune to Jedi Mind Tricks.

advanced stage of preparedness, this will be a time to achieve even greater wealth (trading scarce tangibles for more land, vehicles, greater firepower, etc). Let's start developing those bartering and haggling skills now, as this is the type of economy that will evolve, as we head down the rocky road of collapse.

XIX   Electromagnetic Pulse (EMP) and Coronal Mass Ejection (CME)

The reason for my writing of this chapter is due to the fact that we are currently entering the beginning of a cyclical period of solar flare activity, which is expected to become more intense during the 2013-2014 period. In addition, many experts, to include a US Congressional Panel led by Maryland Congressman Roscoe Bartlett (who also happens to be a hero among the Peak Oil community) have outlined the vulnerabilities within the US to non-direct nuclear attack, consisting of high altitude detonations of nuclear weapons, which in turn generate the atmospheric chain reaction known as Electromagnetic Pulse, or EMP.

To explain briefly what EMP is, it is radio wave-like energy that is emitted from a nuclear detonation. As a direct hit on a physical target, nuclear detonations only produce a limited amount of EMP. However, a nuclear device, detonated, high in the atmosphere (or above), can produce an electrical chain-reaction, affecting everything below it, line-of-sight. This energy is usually expressed in, and measured in the tens, to hundreds of thousands of volts. The same goes for a coronal mass ejection, or CME, from our Sun.

Electromagnetic Pulse can effect entire power grids, as well as anything solid-state (semiconductors, transistors, integrated circuits, etc.), particularly if it has an antenna connected. Regardless of this, the EMP wave will generally hit any and all circuitry at the same time, unless it is specifically shielded against it. This energy can vary in strength once a chain-reaction sets-up in the atmosphere. The energy, measured in volts, can range from a few thousand, to millions of volts of EMP. Therefore, if the Earth takes a hit, a likely scenario could be all of the power lines taking a hit (since they act like big antennas for EMP), but automobiles could still functioning. Tests conducted at the US Army's White Sands Missile Range with their own EMP generator indicated that the average automobile could actually take upwards of roughly 50,000 volts of EMP, and actually be restarted, if knocked-out. At 60,000 volts and above, the test car used could not be restarted. This is probably due to the fact that most automobiles are already surrounded by a "case ground," a negative-potential covering of metal. This is actually what shields military equipment: A metal case surrounding the unit that is negatively grounded.

A massive power disrupting event has already occurred in recent times, during the CME-induced power outage that took place in March of 1989 in Quebec, Canada. Because of massively long power lines which acted like a huge antenna, electrical power was knocked out for millions of people for roughly nine hours. Vehicles and other stand-alone electronic devices were not affected, however.

The biggest fear among experts on this issue is the occurrence of another "Carrington Effect." This was the largest CME event ever in recorded history that occurred at the beginning of September, 1859. It created the most massive geomagnetic storm ever recorded. Telegraph stations and lines were severely damaged, with telegraph stations actually catching fire, and electrically shocking telegraph operators throughout Europe and North America.

Without going into much detail, it is pretty obvious that with our modern infrastructure so heavily dependent on the power grid, imagine a world-wide, or hemispherical collapse of the power grid, with no expectation of repair for at least three years. If this occurs, that is pretty much it for the 10,000 year experiment of human civilization. A die-off measured in billions would then commence.

A book that I highly recommend, and once did a widely-viewed review of, is the novel *One Second After*, about a rogue nation EMP attack on the United States. If Jim Rawles' *Patriots* became the modern bible of survivalism, then William R. Forstchen's *One Second After* would have to be the same on the subject of the effects of an EMP, or possibly a CME event (In the case of even a major CME event, we may still have operating vehicles, as well as individual electronic devices, equipment, etc. However, backup power for nuclear power plants could fail, leading to complete nuclear meltdowns, according to Matthew Stein, the MIT-educated author of *When Technology Fails*.).

The human die-off in *One Second After* occurs in waves. The first to go are all of the nursing home residents, as they lose their medications (particularly the ones that require refrigeration), dietary needs, etc. Next are all the people on various other medications, people suffering from their own obesity and lives of over-consumption, etc. The author also does a good job conveying how pampered and spoiled a society we've been, with medications for everything: Keeping people alive in a state that was never originally intended for human beings, such as drug-coated stints, and other heart medications, in particular. One reference is made to a 41-year old, who dies from a heart attack, simply carrying a bucket of water to his house. He is described as "50-pounds overweight, with cholesterol of 280", and was known to live off of fast food.

To make a long story short, The US begins to resemble Somalia, as things go from bad to worse in this novel.

The best way to prep for an EMP / CME event is to store *all* of your non-regularly used electronics items in "Faraday cages," meaning sealed metal containers, either metal cans or Mylar bags that have complete electrical continuity, meaning that electrical energy cannot penetrate it. Initially, you will want to put your devices in a Ziploc, or bubble wrap bag, etc. as an insulative (non-conducting) layer within the can, Mylar bag, or aluminum foil. Surplus ammunition cans are excellent for use as EMP boxes. Just make sure that you have electrical continuity at both ends of the lid, and the rest of the can.

You also want to already have a system in place where you can not only preserve food, but put it up in long-term storage, without the use of electrical input. The dehydration methods and Mason jar vacuum sealing method for storing food mentioned earlier in this book are a good example.

We don't know when a serious EMP or CME event will occur, or if one will even occur within our lifetimes. However, the effects could be beyond catastrophic. It would definitely be an instant, civilization-ending event. If we ever do have a situation like the novel *One Second After*, anyone with any electronic devices still functioning, particularly any modern vehicles, will literally be viewed in a god-like, envied status.

Conclusion

Obviously, I could have added more material to this book, in more detailed areas, such as forms of transportation (pre and post-collapse), the set-up of early warning devices and booby traps (a disclaimer is appropriate for this subject, as the actual placement of devices designed to inflict injury or death are felonies in most states, although there is nothing wrong with practicing their set-up, *and* recovery), group tactics, shooting skills, etc. I wanted to reach a specific audience, which happens to be the general public, who are just now starting to get a clue. I also intended this book as a good review guide, for those more familiar with preparedness. I hope that it was entertaining, as well.

The US Army uses a stage-based training concept known as "crawl, walk, run." A lot of this book was written for the crawl and walk-phases. This is a great metaphor, since as survivalists we will need to know how to crawl, and spend a lot of time walking, literally. The run-phase would have been subjects like what vehicles will work best in the future, along with squad tactics, more detail into defendability, and more detailed time spent on the subjects of unarmed combat, etc.

I'm not exactly a psychic, but if I were to break out a crystal ball, it would be based on current trends.

Greece, Spain, Portugal and Italy are continuing to implode, a symptom of the global debt crisis. The UK and the US are already following in their footsteps. Greece, in particular, is now denuding its forests, as the populace switches from oil and natural gas, to legal, and illegal means of obtaining firewood for woodstoves and inefficient fireplaces, in order to stay warm.

Here in the US, the US Federal Government is making its own preparations for economic collapse. The new internal security apparatus ("Homeland" Security) of the US Government has been stockpiling massive quantities of particularly lethal (hollow-point) pistol ammunition, and other supplies.

Even more ominous, the revelations of whistleblowers such as Edward Snowden and Bradley Manning are making the US Federal Government desperate at this point, as it is becoming more recognized (domestically *and* internationally) as a tyrant, a bully, and the latest "evil empire" in civilized history.

Suicide rates have exploded in Greece and Spain. Suicide in the US has now (as of 2010) surpassed auto accident deaths (and this is not counting other forms of accidental death, where coroners are unable to determine intent). As a former military man, I can vouch for the fact that the military has always been a microcosm of the society at-large. Over the decades, drugs (1960's and '70's), body weight, and more recently, suicide, have been major issues. As a progressive member of the military, and a radical thinker (from its Latin root, meaning "the root of"), I knew that one of the main reasons for the levels of suicide was that many young people who had never previously entertained the thought of joining the military were now in situations where they were completely hopeless, as economic opportunities in the civilian sector have remained relatively bleak.[10] The military itself has never wanted to acknowledge this. It all reminds me of the Cormack McCarthy novel *The Road*, where in a flashback scene from earlier, after the event,[11] the husband and wife discuss suicide, as their neighbors had already done.

The only predictions that I feel comfortable in making are long-term ones, regarding the rest of this century, based on an adult lifetime of research, and fusion between a multitude of sources:

---

[10]   Arguably, under the artificial economic stimulus known as Quantitative Easing, *some* higher-paying jobs have been created, as of 2013.

[11]   Presumably a nuclear exchange, based on a Cormack McCarthy interview.

- That global economic growth, as we understand it, will end by 2030.

- That by mid-century, global reserves of oil will be largely depleted. Coal and natural gas will have peaked by this time and going into their rates of production decline, exacerbated by the depletion of oil (coal used in coal-to-liquids conversion, which is still currently a very inefficient process, natural gas substitution, etc.). At the time of this writing, there is an abominable PR campaign, suggesting that the US may once again become energy self-reliant, and a net fossil fuel exporter. This was the same garbage going around when the Alaskan Pipeline was being built in the 1970's. The peak for US oil production still stands at roughly 9.5 mbl/d, as of December, 1970 (US EIA). This type of lying, this far into the game, reminds me of the movie *Soylent Green*, where the big terrible secret was that the oceans were already dead, and that the "Soylent Green" food, which was supposed to be coming from plankton, was actually coming from somewhere else (still to this day, the most depressing film I have ever seen in my life)...

- That climate change, in itself, will alter the future of mankind. Global average temperatures have already risen roughly one degrees Celsius, since the start of the industrial age. This is an anomalous measure, outside the normal range of temperatures for the last 1000 years. More areas of the planet will become uninhabitable, with other areas suffering unpredictable weather extremes (both heating *and* cooling). It has also been reported, as of 2013 that we are now at 400 ppm (parts per million) of carbon dioxide (CO_2) in the atmosphere. This is the highest reading of CO_2 level within the last 300,000 years. Many climate scientists explain that the last 10,000 years of human civilization was due largely to unusually stable global weather. Various international agencies are also predicting as much as a three, or four degree rise in average global temperature, by the middle of this century. This basically means flooded major coastal cities, land salinization, and possibly what *some* scientists now call Near-Term Extinction (aka, "NTE") of the human species, by mid-century.[12]

- That a human die-off will commence this century, resulting in a "bottleneck," where more physically healthy, adaptable and ethically advanced people will survive. In other words, a society that once again learns to maintain an equilibrium with its environment, regardless of its level of technological sophistication. This has happened before in pre-history, where the human population in Africa was once reduced to as few as roughly 200 mating pairs.

One item that would be irresponsible not to address, with regards to preparedness and survivalism is the issue of ethnicity and race. I wanted to wait until this chapter to mention it, because I did not want to appear as someone who differentiates, based on ethnicity, culture, etc. This is currently an important issue, because the entire doomer spectrum, from neo-hippies to hardcore survivalists, seems to be culturally dominated by baby boomer-aged white people, who may inadvertently be conveying the message, "We're just trying to save our own (older) white asses" (after all, they were the ones who began the back-to-the-land and survivalism movements, back in the 1970's). I hope that this is not the actual perceived case among traditional minorities in this country, as everyone that I know personally within the preparedness movement are all-inclusive, and have no issues with race or ethnicity (and are even concerned themselves, with this

---

[12]   Dr. Guy McPherson has been a cheerleader of this concept regarding global warming-induced human extinction, drawing on the flawed research of Malcolm Light, an eccentric with no actual climatological experience.

potential image).

Jim Kunstler, author of *The Long Emergency* and the fictional companion *World Made by Hand* simply assumes that if we do indeed have a fast crash, that there will be wars between different societal groups (I've met Kunstler myself at a peak oil conference, and he really is a bitter curmudgeon, despite what he tries to convey in his interviews). Nicole Foss of *The Automatic Earth* website, has generally alluded to the same thing based on her historical knowledge of societal breakdown, citing the intolerance that was generated by key war criminals, prior to the Bosnian War, as an example.

If anything, the preparedness movement within the U.S. *needs* the expertise of different ethnicities, from the people of Bosnia, to the people who somehow managed to survive the Khmer Rouge of 1970's Cambodia. I hope that anyone who is reading this book, and considers themselves a minority makes the effort to network with other preppers and survivalists. If and when a complete societal breakdown comes, I hope that we as a people are ethically advanced enough within the US, to where societal differences are not an issue. When I traveled to Libya in 2011, it was not for any ideological reasons, other than to experience a war in the tradition of Earnest Hemingway, and to see if I could help-out a group of people whose backs were against the wall, at that time. As a matter of fact, I noticed how in the later stages of the Libyan war, as the rebel army became more structured, there was a blend of Christians, Muslims, and various Libyan ethnicities integrated into the various units. Needless to say, this was never reported by the mainstream media. I never witnessed any intolerance between the Libyan people.

Even if nothing of consequence happens in your region of the country / world for a few more generations, let's look at the other reasons for being a survivalist:

- Being physically fit is fun!

- Being as self-reliant as possible, and giving the finger to an exploitive (and increasingly totalitarian) culture of make-believe (primarily here in the U.S.) is fun!

- Gardening, and growing your own food is fun!

- Target shooting, and other firearms-related activities are fun!

- Knowing that you're prepared for any foreseen emergency is a very empowering feeling.

As Charles Eisenstein mentioned in *The Ascent of Humanity*, pre-civilizational humans living in tribal arrangements (which is still the ideally sized community for us humans) had reason to be happy, as their activities were all subsistence-oriented: Hunting and fishing, along with early horticulture (gardening) replacing nomadic hunting and gathering. For us modern, "civilized" human beings, we now pay money for most of these activities, as they are now seen purely as recreation. All this, in addition to a strong community consisting of family, relatives, and neighbors. And we wonder why our current Umerican society suffers from depression, suicide, drug abuse and incarceration. Our current civilization does not give many people an environment in which to enjoy their lives.

So, even if nothing bad ever happens in your lifetime, it's still fun to be a prepper!

Bibliography

Austerity Policy Destroying Greek Society. (2012, February 16). *Nakedcapitalism.com*. Retrieved from http://www. nakedcapitalism.com/ 2012/02/austerity-policy- destroying-greek-society.html.

Benson, Ragnar. (1999). *Ragnar's Guide to the Underground Economy*. Boulder, CO. Paladin Press.

Blumenthal, Dale. (n.d.). The Canning Process: Old Preservation Technique Goes Modern. Retrieved from: http://web.archive. org/web/20070509153848/http://www.fda.gov/bbs/ topics/ CONSUMER/CON00043.html.

Campbell, Steve. (2010) *American Apocalypse II: Refuge*. Flying Turtles of Doom Press.

Curtis, Adam (Producer, Director & Writer) with Lucy Kelsall and Stephen Lambert (Associate Producers) (2002). *Century of the Self*. BBC Four. Documentary retrieved from http://topdocumentaryfilms.com/the-century-of-the-self/.

Department of the Army (1968). *Camouflage* (FM 5-20). Baltimore, MD. US Army AG Publications Center.

Diamond, Jared (2011). *Collapse: How Societies Choose to Fail or Succeed*. Penguin Books. Revised Edition.

Dominguez, Joe & Robin, Vicki. (1992). *Your Money or Your Life*. New York. Viking Press.

Eisenstein, Charles. (2007). *The Ascent of Humanity: The Age of Separation, the Age of Reunion, and the Convergence of Crises that is Birthing the Transition*. Harrisburg, PA. Panenthea Press.

Gannon, Megan. (2013). Suicide Now Kills More Americans Than Car Crashes. *Livescience.com*. Retrieved from http://www.livescience.com/23432-suicide-kills-more-than-car-crashes.html.

Genzlinger, Neil (2012, March 11). Doomsday Has Its Day in the Sun. *The New York Times*. Retrieved from http://www.nytimes.com/2012/03/12/arts/television/doomsday-preppers-and-doomsday-bunkers-tv-reality- shows.html.

German, Erik (2012, June 24). $5B CAMO SNAFU: Army Ditches Failed Combat Uniform That Put a Target on Grunts' Backs for Eight Years. *The Daily.com*. Retrieved from http://www.thedaily. com/ page/2012/06/ 24/062412-news-camouflage-fiasco-1-5/.

Griffith, Justin (2012, February 8). How Nat Geo Misrepresented the Foxhole Atheist 'Doomsday Prepper,' Megan Hurwitt. *Freethought Blogs.com*. Retrieved from http://freethoughtblogs.com/rockbeyondbelief/2012/02/08/how-nat-geo-misrepresented-the-foxhole-atheist-doomsday-prepper-megan-hurwitt/.

Gini Coefficient. (n.d.). Wikipedia. Retrieved from http://en.wikipedia.org/wiki/Gini_coefficient.

Greer, John Michael. (2008). *The Long Descent: A User's Guide to the End of the Industrial Age*. New Society Publishers.

International Space Station. (n.d.). Retrieved from Wikipedia: http://en.wikipedia.org/wiki/International_Space_Station.

Karnow, Stanley (1997). *Vietnam: A History*. 2nd Edition. Penguin.

Kresge, Naomi (2012, January 10). Greek Crisis Has Pharmacists Pleading for Aspirin as Drug Supply Dries Up. *Bloomberg*. Retrieved from http://www.bloomberg.com/news/2012-01-

10/greek-crisis-has-pharmacists-pleading-for-aspirin-as-drug-supply-dries-up.html.

Kermeliotis, Teo (2012, April 6). Austerity drives up suicide rate in debt-ridden Greece. *CNN*. Retrieved from http://www.cnn.com/ 2012/04/ 06/world/europe/greece-austeritysuicide/ index.html?hpt=hp_c2.

Pucket, Dean (Producer, Director & Editor) and Ahmed, Nafeez Mosaddeq (Writer & Presenter) (2011). *The Crisis of Civilization*. Documentary retrieved from http:// crisisofcivilization.com/watch/.

Pugsley, John A (1980). *The Alpha Strategy: The Ultimate Plan of Financial Self-Defense*. Retrieved from http://www. biorationalinstitute.com/zcontent/alpha_strategy. PDF.

Rawles, James Wesley, (2009). *Patriots: A Novel of Survival in the Coming Collapse*. Berkeley, CA. Ulysses Press.

Romney, Edward H. (2001). *Living Well on Practically Nothing*: *Revised and Updated*. Boulder, CO. Paladin Press.

Schifrin, Nick (2011, December 30). Was Teen Killed By CIA Drone a Militant -- or Innocent Victim? *ABC News*. Retrieved from http://abcnews.go.com/Blotter/tariq-khan-killed-cia- drone/story?id=15258659#.UFHy3MjLdDp.

Squires, Nick (2012). Young Italians flock to become shepherds. *The Telegraph*. Retrieved from http://www.telegraph.co. uk/finance/jobs/9244441/Young-Italians-flock-to-become-shepherds.html.

The Fallacy of Bugging Out. (2012, April 18). *Survival Acres.com*. Retrieved from http://survivalacres.com/blog/the-fallacy-of-bugging-out.

Joe Snuffy In Misrata, Libya, June, 2011

About the Author

"Joe Snuffy" is a preparedness author and consultant who specializes in both the self-reliance and tactical aspects of preparedness. He traveled to Libya at the peak of their revolutionary war as a freelance journalist. Snuffy has been featured in TIME Magazine, CNN, and National Public Radio. In addition to his B.A. Degree in Intelligence Studies and A.A.S. Degree in Electronics Technology, he is also a noted Peak Oil, civilizational decline, and collapse theorist. Snuffy has written for *Survivalist* and *Soldier of Fortune* magazines, as well as various websites, such as SurvivalBlog.com, EnergyBulletin.net, and CultureChange.org.

www.ingramcontent.com/pod-product-compliance
Lightning Source LLC
Chambersburg PA
CBHW070001300526
45794CB00001B/139